VISCOUNT BOLINGBROKE

STUDIES IN POLITICAL HISTORY

Editor: Michael Hurst
Fellow of St. John's College, Oxford

VISCOUNT BOLINGBROKE

Tory Humanist

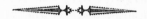

by

JEFFREY HART

Associate Professor of English
Dartmouth College

LONDON: Routledge & Kegan Paul
TORONTO: University of Toronto Press
1965

First published 1965
in Great Britain by
Routledge & Kegan Paul Ltd
and in Canada by
University of Toronto Press

Printed in Great Britain by
W. & J. Mackay & Co Ltd

CONTENTS

v

PREFACE

THIS study of Henry St. John, Viscount Bolingbroke, owes much to the encouragement and perceptive criticism of Professors James L. Clifford and Marjorie Nicolson of Columbia University. A generous grant from the Columbia University Committee on Research in the Humanities permitted me to undertake research in England which uncovered a number of previously unfamiliar details concerning Bolingbroke's career. The staff of the British Museum was most helpful. Another grant from the Dartmouth College Committee on Research greatly assisted in the preparation of the manuscript. I wish to acknowledge my gratitude.

I desire to dedicate this book to my parents.

JEFFREY HART

Goodrich-Four-Corners, Vermont

INTRODUCTION

BOLINGBROKE's reputation suffered a sharp decline after his death in 1751, and Burke's estimate, implicit in his famous rhetorical question, 'Who now reads Bolingbroke?' has been valid ever since. We can best appreciate the extent of the decline when we recall the opinion of his powers entertained by his most intelligent contemporaries. 'Nothing can depress his genius,' wrote Pope. 'Whatever befalls him, he will still be the greatest man in the world, either in his own time, or with posterity.'[1] Swift reported to Stella in November 1711 that St. John, then Secretary of State at the extraordinary age of 33, was 'the greatest young man I ever knew; wit, capacity, beauty, quickness of apprehension, good learning, and an excellent taste; the best orator in the House of Commons . . .' Lord Chesterfield agreed completely. Bolingbroke, he said, 'adorned whatever subject he either spoke or wrote upon by the most splendid eloquence; not a studied or laboured eloquence, but such a glowing happiness of diction, which (from care perhaps at first) is become so habitual, that even his most familiar conversations, if taken down in writing, would have borne the press, without the least correction, either as to method or style'.[2] Thomas Jefferson thought Bolingbroke's style approached perfection: 'Lord Bolingbroke's . . . is a style of the highest order. The lofty, rhythmical, full flowing eloquence of Cicero. Periods of just measure, their numbers proportioned, their close full and round. His conceptions, too, are bold and strong, his diction copious, polished and commanding as his subject. His writings are certainly the finest examples in the English language of the eloquence proper for the Senate.'[3] And the younger Pitt remarked that of all the lost intellectual treasures of the world he would like to see recovered a speech of Bolingbroke's.[4]

[1] *The Correspondence of Alexander Pope*, ed. George Sherburn (Oxford, 1956).
[2] D. G. James, *The Life of Reason* (London, 1949), p. 196.
[3] Saul K. Padover, *A Jefferson Profile* (New York, 1956), p. 316.
[4] D. G. James, p. 196.

Bolingbroke's subsequent disrepute owes much to his religious scepticism, but still more to the fact that he was on the losing side politically. For the anger his posthumously published religious views could arouse, we have only to think of Johnson's detonation: 'Sir, he was a scoundrel, and a coward; a scoundrel for charging a blunderbuss against religion and morality; a coward because he had no resolution to fire it off himself, but left half a crown to a beggarly Scotchman to draw the trigger after his death.' Bolingbroke's reputation also has suffered because until recently history has been written mainly by Whigs. John Morley, a pure specimen of the type, wrote in 1889 that 'of all the characters in our history, Bolingbroke must be pronounced to be most of a charlatan; of all the writing in our literature, his is the hollowest, the flashiest, the most insincere', and that 'Bolingbroke's methods must be stamped by every impartial historian with indelible infamy'.[5] This is the typical estimate of Bolingbroke, and it has echoed through the history books for a century and a half. As the Whig certitudes have faded, however, our understanding of the Tory position has deepened, as has our sympathy for those who wrote from a Tory point of view. And sympathy has led to knowledge. Only recently, for example, has sufficient account been taken of the connection of such writers as Swift, Pope, and Gay, with the humanist tradition of the Renaissance. Not only does *Gulliver's Travels* allude ironically to prominent features of the work of More and Rabelais—the imaginary voyage, the utopia, the satirical use of giants and diminutive men; it also defends in a variety of ways their humanist ethos. Similarly, *The Dunciad* scourges those who in Pope's opinion were subverting humanist values, and also suggests through elaborate rhetorical techniques the positive cultural values to be defended. It has not been recognised that in *The Idea of a Patriot King* Bolingbroke was employing a similar strategy, and writing a 'manual for the prince', a work in the *de regimine principum* tradition as practised by Erasmus, Elyot, Patricius, Budé, Beroaldus, Machiavelli, and many others. One of the principal aims of this study, therefore, will be to show how Bolingbroke, like the more familiar writers who were associated with him, was concerned to attack from the point of view of the humanist tradition of the Renaissance

[5] John Morley, *Walpole* (London, 1889), p. 25.

those complex forces which in retrospect we may view as marking the advent of 'modernity'. Like Swift, Pope, and Gay, Bolingbroke inherited cultural assumptions, reflected in a comprehensive cultural style, which had long been taken for granted—considered, that is, 'natural' or 'rational'. And like them he confronted a circumstance in which these values were under powerful attack. By re-examining Bolingbroke and his work in the context of his time, we may come to share something of the high regard his contemporaries had for him, and perhaps even discard Morley's estimate for that of T. S. Eliot: Bolingbroke was 'a master of prose, whose work can no more be ignored by the student of English literature than by the student of politics'.[6]

The high public style of the Augustans, and the values implicated in it, provided the basis for an international civilisation which, since the French Revolution, has ceased to exist. From the perfect to the preposterous, from Pope's couplets and Jefferson's Monticello to *Irene* or, worse, the blank-verse dramas of Custis, in which every hero is an alabaster Washington with a name like Marcus Tullius Scipio Americanus,[7] a broad cultural consensus manifested itself in an agreement upon style. There is a sense in which Bolingbroke, sitting in exile at Chantelou and writing on the decline of nations, and a young backwoods Virginian of the 1760s like Thomas Jefferson, were the noblest Romans of them all. The high public style, which the Augustans had inherited from their humanist predecessors of the Renaissance, was, in its intent, a guarantee of disinterestedness. It was a way of making public one's detachment from the lower motives: economic gain, physical comfort, personal survival at any cost. It constituted an affirmation of one's imaginative involvement with the well-being of the State. It was thus a style designed for a ruling class.

During the first half of the eighteenth century such continuators of the humanist tradition as Swift, Pope, Gay, and Bolingbroke make strategic reference to one or more of the characteristic humanist *genres* in order to assert polemically the style and the values of a ruling class at the moment of its disintegration.

[6] T. S. Eliot, 'The Literature of Politics' (London, 1955), p. 12.
[7] Allen Tate, 'What Is a Traditional Society?' in *On the Limits of Poetry* (New York, 1948), pp. 294–304.

They reflected in their works, indeed, one of the great turning-points of modern history. Heretofore the values operative in Western culture had been the traditional ones associated with Christianity and the classics. With the Tory humanists, such traditional values become in some part *critical*, modes of attack upon other values that are beginning to prevail. Everyone has sensed a revolutionary component in Swift, in his indignation and outrage—not, one sees, typically conservative emotions. The same is true, though in lesser degree, of his associates. Brecht's use of Gay is significant in this connection. To put it simply, what happened in the course of the eighteenth century was that the traditional conception of society, giving way before the commercial and then the industrial revolutions, became a component of the politics of protest. In *The Deserted Village*, notably, the speaker preserves the Augustan manner, but speaks *from the point of view of the lower classes*. The career of Cobbett is a kind of paradigm. Beginning as a disciple of Burke, and always attached to the values of a traditional society, he became an intransigeant critic of early nineteenth-century industrial society. Perhaps the process is best described this way: in defeat, the traditional position undergoes fragmentation. Part of it, as in Cobbett, becomes actively revolutionary; another part, as in Arnold and Eliot, becomes a critique of modernity from the point of view of culture or religion.

We may take it as symbolic of this transformation of tradition that most of Bolingbroke's life, his entire career after the death of Anne, was devoted to *opposition*. He was one of the first to recognise clearly the nature of the new forces that were ascendant in politics. At the time of the Glorious Revolution, he writes, 'few people . . . foresaw how the creation of funds, and the multiplication of taxes, would increase yearly the power of the crown . . . The notion of attaching men to the new government by tempting them to embark their fortunes on the same bottom, was a reason of state to some: the notion of creating a new, that is, a moneyed interest, in opposition to the landed interest, and of acquiring a superior influence in the city of London at least by the establishment of great corporations, was a reason of party to others . . . They looked no farther.'[8] This last sentence epitomises, in as few words as it is

[8] *The Works of Lord Bolingbroke*, II (Philadelphia, 1841), pp. 187–8.

possible to do so, the criticism Bolingbroke and the other Tory humanists were making of the new men of their time: *they looked no farther*. No farther than immediate gain. They were unfit to rule.

It is the seriousness, the critical awareness, of the Tory humanists that distinguishes them from such lesser classicising writers as Thomson, Akenside, Churchill, and even Addison. They knew that their classicism was not only a manner but a system of values, and that, as it had evolved in England since the sixteenth century, it was inextricable from the kind of society that had produced it. The humanist ethos could not inform a more complex society characterised by commerce, individualism, urban social mobility, and increasingly subjective moral standards. In the Tory humanists awareness of conflict gave edge to their satire and sharpened their invective. They knew that their style, and the forms they chose, implied particular values. And so, in contrast to innumerable classicising contemporaries, they could not employ that style as an ornament. They used it as a weapon.

I

THE HUMANIST BACKGROUND

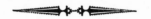

A PAINTING attributed to Melozzo da Forli, and now in the Queen's collection at Windsor, brings before us a scene which embodies one of the most important ideals of the Renaissance. The Duke of Urbino, Federigo da Montefeltro, wearing his robes of State, sits in a large rectangular hall, his left hand resting on a folio. Guidobaldo, his son, about 11 years old and dressed in yellow damask trimmed with pearls, stands at the Duke's knee. Behind the Duke and his son, on a raised platform with a desk before it, sit three men. One wears the red suit of a prelate; the second, black ecclesiastical garb; the third, secular clothes. Servants and courtiers stand near by unobtrusively. All are listening with great attention to a grey-haired humanist, dressed in black robes, who sits in a pulpit opposite the Duke. Open on the desk before him is a large book bound in crimson and adorned with silver clasps. We see that the humanist is reading aloud to his distinguished audience, no doubt from some classical or Christian author, and, as was the practice, commenting on the text as he proceeds.[1]

It is the humanist who is in the pulpit. The man of letters instructs not only the head of State, the Duke, but also the clergyman and the courtier in the background. This scene at the Court of Urbino thus reflects an assumption central to the humanist programme and to the culture of the Renaissance— that education, a literary education derived in large part from classical sources, might succeed where the medieval curriculum no longer seemed quite adequate, might succeed in establishing

---

[1] John Addington Symonds, *Renaissance in Italy: the Revival of Learning* (London, 1882), pp. 304–7.

a just social order and in taming the dark impulses in men's hearts. The scene in the painting epitomises another truth about the humanist programme: it was aristocratic in character, devised for the governing class. The servants in the painting are mere lookers-on. The humanists of the Renaissance considered, not without reason, that a principled, educated ruling class was the key to the good society. These humanist assumptions were central to European educated culture from the fifteenth through the eighteenth century, the eighteenth century being, in Alfred North Whitehead's excellent phrase, the silver age of the European Renaissance. Indeed, a principal concern of recent scholarship has been to explore the relationship of such writers as Dryden, Swift, Pope, and Gay to the humanist tradition.[2]

Bolingbroke himself saw quite clearly his own connection with the Renaissance. Letter VI of *On the Study and Use of History* advises the prospective administrator to study carefully only the history of the period since the 'resurrection of letters'. What happened before, during the Middle Ages, was so different that it would have little educational value for the statesman: 'to be learned about them is a ridiculous affectation in any man who means to be useful to the present age'.[3] But the subsequent era, that of the Renaissance, is intimately connected with Bolingbroke's own period:

> But a new system of causes and effects, that subsists in our time, and whereof our conduct is to be a part, arising at the last period i.e., the Renaissance, and all that passes in our time being dependent on what has passed since that period, or being immediately relative to it, we are extremely concerned to be well informed about all these passages.[4]

He concedes that to be entirely ignorant of the Middle Ages 'would be shameful', and endorses a 'temperate curiosity' toward them. But it is the Renaissance that seems to him primary. In his opinion the modern era began in the reign of Henry VII: 'Our temple of Janus was shut by Henry the Seventh. We neither laid waste our own nor other countries any longer: and

---

[2] See, for example, Ian Jack, *Augustan Satire* (Oxford, 1952); Aubrey Williams, *Pope's Dunciad* (London, 1955); Bernard Schilling, *Dryden and the Conservative Myth* (New Haven, 1961); Sven Armens, *John Gay: Social Critic* (New York, 1954).

[3] *The Works of Lord Bolingbroke*, II (Philadelphia, 1841), p. 239.

[4] Ibid.

wise laws and a wise government changed insensibly the manners, and gave a new turn to the spirit of our people.'[5]

Perhaps the most important way in which the humanist programme differed from that of the medieval curriculum was in its emphasis upon the public world. It tried to re-imagine the public career, endow it with dignity and significance, and we may easily suppose that this was because the nation, and even the Empire, were once again becoming available as imaginative possibilities. Administrators were needed, perhaps more than saints and warriors. The humanist educators of the Renaissance tended to regard the medieval curriculum, and medieval culture generally, as centred on private things. One might devote oneself to contemplation, or else debate interminably a series of arcane propositions, yet none of these activities seemed to have much to do with the business at hand. The humanist programme as it developed had at its centre not a contemplative life but an active one, and not a series of propositions but the image of a certain kind of person. That image was drawn in large part from the classical ideal of the orator. For Cicero, as for Ascham or Bolingbroke, the true orator is the man of universal knowledge who is able to apply his wisdom to political practice. Language is supremely important to him, for it is the medium through which private knowledge must be made publicly available: it is the public face of wisdom. From the point of view of the humanist, his medieval opponents were to be condemned not so much because they were wrong as because their truth, if it were truth, was so specialised as to be incommunicable.[6] They are dead as far as the public life is concerned.

[5] Ibid., p. 245.

[6] See *Gargantua and Pantagruel*, trans. J. M. Cohen (Penguin, 1957), Ch. 19, also p. 70: 'The Sophist read him the *Compostum*, on which he spent sixteen years and two months. . . . In the year fourteen twenty he caught the pox.'

The continuity of ethical assumption between the sixteenth and the eighteenth centuries is exemplified by passages like the following from Ascham's *The Scholemaster* (1570), which would serve very well as a gloss upon Book Three of *Gulliver's Travels*:

Some wittes, moderate enough by nature, be many tymes marde by over moch studie and use of some sciences, namelie, Musicke, Arithmetick, and Geometrie. Thies sciences, as they sharpen mens wittes over moch, so they change mens maners over sore, if they be not moderatlie mingled, & to som good use of life. Marke all mathematicall heades, which be onely and wholy bent to those sciences, how solitarie they be themselves, how unfit to live with others, & how unapt to serve in the world.

(Roger Ascham, *English Works*, ed. Wm. A. Wright (Cambridge, 1904), p. 190.)

3

It is not to be supposed, however, that because the humanists stressed the utility of knowledge the humanist programme was therefore narrowly utilitarian. The kind of person they wished to produce, like Cicero's orator, must master a wide range of knowledge, for otherwise his attempts at eloquence would result, as Cicero had warned, in 'but an empty and ridiculous swirl of verbiage'.[7] The orator, that is the statesman or senator, must be a student of human nature, a master of psychology: 'all the human emotions, with which nature has endowed the human race, are to be intimately understood, because it is in calming or kindling the feelings of the audience that the full power and science of oratory are to be brought into play'.[8] The orator must know 'the complete history of the past', as well as attain 'a knowledge of all important subjects and arts', and in particular of moral philosophy.[9] Eloquence, language—perhaps one could now say poetry—is the way in which the knowledge of the specialist is made relevant to life as it is lived. The mind the humanists wished to create would be able to synthesise the various kinds of knowledge, and awareness, that made up the culture that had produced it.

The distinctive thing about the humanist tradition is that the poet, the historian, and the moral philosopher, no less than the speaker in the forum, conceived themselves to be public figures. As indeed they were, if one thinks of More, Ascham, Spenser, and Milton. They really were 'advisers to the prince', and it would not have seemed fatuous to them to take as their exemplar the archetypal poet of Horace's *Art of Poetry*: 'Orpheus, seer and bard in one, weaned savage forest tribes from murder and foul living; whence the legend that he tamed tigers and fierce lions . . . This was the poets' wisdom of old—to draw a line between man and the state, the sacred and the common; to build cities, to check promiscuous lust, to assign rights to the married, to engrave laws on wood.'[10] In this tradition the man of letters had a public aspect, and the poet was a man of letters. From Homer and Virgil, from Plutarch, Xenophon,

[7] Cicero, *De oratore*, ed. E. W. Sutton and H. Rackham, I (Cambridge, Mass., 1959), 15.
[8] Ibid.
[9] Ibid., pp. 15, 17.
[10] Horace, *The Complete Works*, ed. Casper J. Kraemer, Jr. (New York, 1936), p. 410.

Tacitus, and Livy, the humanists derived examples of intelligence and courage made active in the service of the State. From Plato, Cicero, and the Christian authors they heard of the life of contemplation. What the humanists found in their tradition was not a consistent body of doctrine but rather a conception of the self, an image of what the heir of the Western tradition ought to be. For the inculcation of their ethos they favoured narrative, whether historical or fictitious, and paid little—too little—attention to systematic philosophy. In the real or fictional lives of great men the apt student could find the essential truth of life, and models to imitate. The *Iliad* had been read in such a way in Hellenistic times.[11] It had been a pedagogic instrument. Virgil was more than a poet for the Renaissance; rather, he *was* a poet, and therefore a teacher. And other writers, in verse or prose, had the same goal in mind: Erasmus and More, Ascham, Elyot, Sydney, Spenser, and Milton, thought of themselves as instructors of the governing class, and, often, of the monarch. The distillation of this attitude was the manual written for the edification of prince or administrator. Such manuals attempted to capture the reader's imagination by presenting to him a vividly conceived ideal of what he ought to be, along with certain precepts about how to approach that ideal. Perhaps the manual represents the humanist's desperation: if the prince or nobleman cannot be improved by his reading of classical poetry, a handbook can be provided him. As examples of manuals of this sort, there come to mind immediately Erasmus's *Institutio principis Christiani*, Budé's *De l'institution du prince*, Castiglione's *Il cortegiano*, and Elyot's *The Governour*. It is true, of course, that medieval writers had also concerned themselves with the character to be desired in a prince, and these Renaissance manuals *de regimine principum* had their medieval predecessors. St. Martin, the Bishop of Bracara (d. 580), addressed to Miro, King of Galicia, a short treatise called *The Formula of an Honourable Life*, in which he recommended the four cardinal virtues as well as a variety of other good qualities. Isidore of Seville (d. 636) gave advice to rulers in the course of writing on other matters, and Alcuin (d. 804) did the same in his epistles. Smaragdus of St. Mihel (d. 830?) wrote a treatise called *Royal Way* which is thought to have been

[11] Moses Hadas, *Humanism: the Greek Ideal and Its Survival* (New York, 1960).

dedicated to Louis the Pious, and Hincemar (d. 882) produced one at the request of Charles the Bald. Peter Damiani (d. 1072) and John of Salisbury (d. 1180?) also wrote on the conduct suitable to a ruler. But the most notable of the medieval works on the subject is undoubtedly the *De regimine principum* of St. Thomas Aquinas (d. 1274), which was written for the King of Cyprus and enjoyed wide popularity, being translated into French, German, and Italian. But despite the fact that medieval writers produced such books of advice for princes, manuals *de regimine principum* may be regarded, both in point of quantity and quality, as a form which flourished during the Renaissance. The manuals written during the Renaissance are longer than their predecessors, are more elaborate and show more concern with literary values, more care in the selection of description and anecdote, and a more sophisticated sense of the competing claims of ethical values and *realpolitik*.

The manual for the prince represented only one among the variety of ways the humanist writer had available to him for the inculcation of desirable values in those who would rule the State. Thus such writers as Sydney, More, Elyot, Ascham, Spenser, Jonson, Milton, Dryden, Swift, Pope, and Bolingbroke conceived of themselves as in some sense pedagogues to the ruler and the ruling class. Erasmus spoke for all writers in this tradition when he said, 'That a Prince be born of worthy character we must beseech the gods above; that a prince born of good parts may not go amiss, or that one of mediocre accomplishments may be bettered through education is mainly within our province.'[12] Many of the writers who so conceived of themselves actually held political office: they were in a literal sense advisers to the prince. But the intellectual efforts of all the writers in the humanist tradition, whether in office or not, were directed toward a single goal: in Milton's words, to 'fit a man to perform justly, skilfully, and magnanimously all the offices both public and private, of peace and war'.[13] This relationship between the writer and the State, between the pedagogue, adviser, and celebrator on the one hand, and the prince or

---

[12] Erasmus, *The Education of a Christian Prince*, ed. Lester K. Born (New York, 1936), pp. 140–1.

[13] John Milton, 'Of Education', *Prose Selections*, ed. Meritt Y. Hughes (New York, 1947), p. 35.

administrator on the other, is central to the humanist tradition; and it thus becomes perfectly clear why, as long as this tradition was alive, as long as this relationship obtained between the writer and the State, the writer could not suppose that his primary function was 'self-expression'. He had other tasks to perform, recognised subject-matter to convey. The writer in the humanist tradition stood in a different relation to his culture than later writers: he created a literature of recognition, rather than of discovery.

Historians agree, generally speaking, that the fifteenth century saw the beginnings of humanism in England.[14] In the early part of the century English humanism was largely a scholarly affair, more concerned with manuscripts and with the technicalities of Ciceronian style than with the promulgation of a humanist vision of life. This may be said even though such works as the *Life of Henry V* by Tito Livio Frulovosi suggest that the moral aspects of humanism were not entirely ignored even in its earliest stages in England. Toward the end of the fifteenth century, however, historical circumstances provided the opportunity for humanism to play a decisive role in the culture at large.

The Tudor monarchy, established in 1485 on the field at Bosworth, greatly centralised English political life. It had come to power at the expense of the feudal barons, and its own support came in considerable degree from the landed gentry. The power the barons had lost gravitated naturally to the Court. The gentry, soon enriched by the seizure of monastery lands, looked to the King for leadership. As the Government thus became more centralised its need increased for a competent civil governing class, and for such a class the medieval conception of the knight, the chivalric ideal of an earlier period, could not provide an appropriate model. Another ideal was far more suitable, and was ready at hand in the classical works which already had some currency in England through the efforts of the Italian humanists. At certain stages of their development, indeed, both Athens and Rome had possessed social structures similar in important respects to that which was emerging in England under the Tudors. In Pericles' Athens and

[14] For the development of English humanism, see especially Fritz Caspari, *Humanism and the Social Order in Tudor England* (Chicago, 1954).

in the Rome of Cicero and Augustus the upper classes dominated the Government, but the State nevertheless had certain republican characteristics. Leading citizens were required to play a responsible role in public affairs, and it was necessary for them to speak, as did Pericles and Cicero, in public assemblies. Under these conditions a gentleman could not hope to play a leading role in affairs if he was only a warrior; and this was becoming the case under the Tudors. The qualities to be desired in a responsible citizen—that he be public-spirited, well educated, eloquent, and graceful as well as dignified in appearance —were summed up in the classical conception of the orator. And because the function of the Tudor governing classes was in many ways similar to that of the Greek and Roman aristocracies, classical ethical ideals could provide useful models for Renaissance education in England, even though the need for oratory was not as great in England as it had been in Greece and Rome. The famous men of these ancient States could provide a pattern for the new administrators of sixteenth-century England.[15]

Italian humanism had its prophet in Petrarch, who dramatised for his contemporaries a decisive rejection of the medieval past and a deliberate turning to the classical past as a model for culture. Erasmus performed the same prophetic function for England. Though Grocyn, Linacre, and Colet had studied in Italy and been influenced by Florentine neoplatonism, it was Erasmus who gave to humanism its imaginative authority. The continuity between the beginning of English humanism and its end, indeed, is suggested by the fact that Erasmus has frequently been said to have been a precursor of eighteenth-century ethical attitudes, and when we compare his characteristic attitudes with those of Pope, Swift, and Bolingbroke we see that this is an accurate estimate. It is significant in this connection, indeed, that the standard edition of his works, the one still used, was printed in the eighteenth century.

Erasmus maintained, as did his successors, including Bolingbroke, that the ethical qualities of the ruler and the ruling class are of decisive importance for the well-being of the State, and— most importantly—that it is the education of the ruler that determines whether he will be a blessing or a curse, a Christian-

15 Caspari, pp. 5–6.

humanist prince or a tyrant. 'It was formerly the custom', writes Erasmus in *The Education of a Christian Prince*, 'to decree statues, arches, and honorary titles to those deserving honour from the state. None is more worthy of this honour than he who labours faithfully and zealously in the proper training of the prince, and looks not to personal emolument but rather to the welfare of his country. A country owes everything to a good prince; him it owes to the man who made him such by moral principles.'[16] This opinion would echo down through the humanist tradition to Bolingbroke's *The Idea of a Patriot King*, and indeed to *Gulliver's Travels*, in which all the unfortunate or wretched societies have been made so by foolish or wicked monarchs, while Brobdingnag has been saved by the wisdom of its monarchs.

Erasmus considered that *ratio*, the rational element in man, was almost synonymous with goodness, and that *ratio* could be made to manifest itself in its highest human form by means of proper education. In Swift's phrase man was 'an animal capable of reason'. The development of the individual's reason by means of education, the bringing to maturity of his potential virtue, would, Erasmus thought, ultimately cause the evolution of just social institutions. One aspect of Bolingbroke's *The Idea of a Patriot King*, as we will see, is its attack upon Machiavelli, and indeed attacks on Machiavellian assumptions are prominent in the works of virtually all the most important and representative English humanists.[17] We find them in Erasmus as well,

[16] *The Education of a Christian Prince*, p. 141.

[17] It has been pointed out here that Erasmus and More, though they had no read the works of Machiavelli, were anti-Machiavellians on the basis of principle, anticipated Machiavelli by attacking the practices he was to recommend. By the time of Elizabeth, however, Englishmen were very much aware of Machiavelli himself. Gentillet's *Discours sur les moyens de bien gouverner*, a violent attack on Machiavelli, appeared in 1576 at Geneva, and was widely read in England. Simon Patericke's translation appeared in 1602, and in the prefatory dedication Patericke gives an example of what was to be the characteristic Elizabethan attitude toward Machiavelli. Queen Elizabeth, 'by maintaining wholesome unitie amongst all degrees, hath hitherto preserved the State of her realm, not onely safe but flourishing, not by Machiavellian artes, as Guile, Perfidie, and other Villanies, practising; but by true vertues, as Clemencie, Justice, Faith. . . . O how happy are yee . . . that the infectious Machiavellian doctrine, hath not breathed nor penetrated the intrails of most happy England.' (Innocent Gentillet, *A Discourse upon the Means of well Governing . . . against Nicholas Machiavelli, the Florentine*, trans. Simon Patericke (London, 1602).

Machiavelli thus was for the humanists something more than an erring political

all the more striking for the fact that Erasmus's attacks preceded the appearance of Machiavelli's works themselves. Some of Erasmus's remarks sound as if they had been written in deliberate polemic against famous assertions of the Florentine. Erasmus's manual *de regimine principum*, his *The Education of a Christian Prince*, thus anticipates not only the form and general moral purpose of Bolingbroke's *The Idea of a Patriot King* but also adumbrates one of its specific ethical endeavours—the assertion of the humanist ideal of *ratio* against Machiavellian *virtu*.[18] The antagonism between the principles of the major English humanists and those of Machiavelli was profound. It was based not only upon different expectations with regard to human nature but also upon different conceptions of the structure of actuality. And when we come to consider Boling-

[18] Many of Erasmus's observations bring to mind famous passages in Machiavelli but by way of contrast. Whereas Machiavelli's prince chooses to be feared rather than loved, Erasmus's Christian prince chooses an opposite course: 'The king rejoices in the freedom of his people; the tyrant strives to be feared, the king to be loved' (*The Education of a Christian Prince*, p. 164). In contrast to Machiavelli's prince, who need only *appear* to be good, and sometimes must *be* evil, the humanist ruler profected by Erasmus, as by Bolingbroke, must be good in fact: 'He must exhibit the highest moral integrity, while in others a general appearance is enough.' Erasmus further maintains 'there can be no good prince who is not also a good man' (ibid., pp. 182, 189).

philosopher. He represented the dark alternative to the ethical standards we have been describing. The man of *virtu*, as conceived by Machiavelli, was seen as a man of power and will, the opposite, that is, of the man bound by *ratio* as the humanists thought of it. It is for this reason that men of heterodox temper, such as Marlowe and Milton, associate their villain-heroes—Tamburlaine, the Jew of Malta, Satan—with Machiavelli. It is 'reason of state', we recall, that Satan offers in justification of his assault on Eden.

In *Mother Hubbard's Tale*, for example, Spenser continues the anti-Machiavellian tradition of his predecessors. This narrative tells how an ape seizes power in the animal kingdom, aided in his rise by the Machiavellian advice of the fox. But the fox claims the throne for himself, arguing that he deserves it because of his 'slie wyles and subtill craftinesse'. Power seized illegitimately, Spenser thus points out, is always unstable, always threatened by rival claims. Caspari has noted here the resemblance between the methods of the fox and practices which were customarily associated with Machiavelli: 'Thus the fox follows Machiavelli's advice by impoverishing the great nobles of the realm, for "he no count made of Nobilitie". He even does away with them by concocting false accusations against them, or else he makes them "dwell in darkness of disgrace". Like the Florentine, the fox is afraid that they may otherwise become too powerful and endanger his rule.' By thus associating Machiavellian precept, as it was generally understood, with the practices of the ape and the fox, traditional symbols of tyranny, Spenser suggests his evaluation of Machiavelli.

broke's *contre-Machiavel* we should remember that opposition to Machiavellian principles, which implied an entire conception of actuality, had always been an important part of the English humanist tradition, had, indeed, antedated Machiavelli.

Erasmus anticipated other attitudes of such eighteenth-century writers as Swift, Pope, and Bolingbroke. Like them he was easily contemptuous of all things medieval, or 'Gothic', and this attitude, indeed, did not cease to be central to high culture until the Gothic revival of the late eighteenth century, which itself was a symptom of humanist decline. Erasmus, placing a high value upon clarity, simplicity, harmony, and reasonableness, execrates the textbooks which had been used for the teaching of Latin when he was young: Mammectractus, Brachylogus, Ebardus—the very names were barbarous to his taste. In the elaborate scholastic systems he saw only sterility, mere exhibitions of ingenuity unrelated to the problems of actual men. The characteristic techniques of medieval literature, particularly symbolism and allegory, seemed ridiculous to him, for he thought the literal meaning of a text ought to be adequate for the meaning to be conveyed. And his contempt for all that he considered ugly, useless, and antiquated—categories that tended to be synonymous for him—embraced virtually all of medieval theology. Huizinga aptly compares his epistles, his treatises, and his *Colloquies*, to a gallery of Brueghel's paintings: through them there passes a procession of ignorant and avaricious monks who hypocritically impose upon the trustful multitude and fare sumptuously themselves.[19] Erasmus's contempt for the medieval past was combined with a certainty that humanist values would triumph. 'The world is coming to its senses,' he wrote, 'as if awakening from a deep sleep. Still there are some left who recalcitrate pertinaciously, clinging convulsively with hands and feet to their old ignorance. They fear that if *bonae litterae* are reborn and the world grows wise, it will come to light that they have known nothing.'[20] When Swift attacks the pedants and the system-builders and the barbarous style of modern literature in *A Tale of a Tub* and *The Battle of the Books*, he is simply substituting the modern enemies of humanism for the medieval ones Erasmus had attacked and helped to defeat. Swift's posi-

[19] J. Huizinga, *Erasmus of Rotterdam* (London, 1952), pp. 100–16.
[20] Ibid., p. 103.

tive values, like those of Erasmus, are the values of Christian humanism. In many ways the great writers of the early eighteenth century recalled Erasmus in their principal works. Erasmus, in order to perfect the literary style, and the manners, of his Christian gentleman, produced a series of pedagogical works. In addition, to prepare the way for his innovating programme, he wrote other works which ridiculed the manners and the intellectual modes of the medieval past. His *Adagia* and his *Copia* provide models of literary style as well as moral instruction; *The Praise of Folly* ridicules the absurdities, really the entire style of life, of the scholastic past. In similar fashion other humanist works, such as the *Epistolae Obscurorum Virorum* and *Gargantua and Pantagruel*, attack the cultural style, the 'ineloquence', of the Middle Ages. Eighteenth-century analogues are obvious. If the humanist attack upon the Middle Ages was conducted mainly in terms of style, the humanist defence against the modern specialist took the same form. The *Peri-Bathous*, the *Memoirs of Martinus Scriblerus*, and the *Dunciad* come at once to mind. The positive values of Swift and Pope, like those of Erasmus, are those of Christian humanism, as that had developed as a tradition during the Renaissance. Erasmus's ideal of culture, as Huizinga says, was the world of antiquity, but illuminated throughout by Christian faith, an 'amalgamation of pure classicism (this meant for him Cicero, Horace, Plutarch; for to the flourishing period of the Greek mind he remained after all a stranger) and pure Biblical Christianity'.[21] Erasmus even argued for the sanctity of certain classical moralists and poets, prayed, indeed, to Socrates—'*Sancte Socrate, pro nobis ora*'—for he was anxious to affirm all of those elements in classical culture which might be interpreted as harmonious with Christianity. And like Dryden, he could not bring himself to believe that the great men of the ancient world would, finally, be damned.[22]

Erasmus, then, may be regarded as the prophet of English humanism, for he gave expression to attitudes that would be found relevant for three centuries, but his ethical vision required the efforts of more practical men to make it firmly a part of English life: men like More, to debate its application to the

[21] Ibid., p. 102.
[22] *Religio Laici*, 11.

world of day-to-day politics,[23] and Colet, to help make it the actual curriculum of the schools. In *The Governour* (1531) Sir Thomas Elyot showed in detail how the humanist ideal could be adapted to the various administrative and judicial roles the gentry were called upon to fulfil. Other less well-known humanists made important contributions to the tradition. Thomas Starkey, for example, stressed the importance of law,

[23] The arguments of Raphael Hythlodaye in the *Utopia* might have been those More had actually heard from Erasmus. Hythlodaye points out that Plato himself had failed when he ventured into practical politics, and argues that the philosopher who participates in government, who becomes an advisor at Court, will at the very least appear ridiculous to men of affairs or, even worse, be himself corrupted by the world. Hythlodaye supports his position by giving a description of politics at the Court of the French King:

> Go to, suppose that I were with the French king, and there sitting in his council, while in that most secret consultation, the king himself there being present in his own person, they beat their brains and search the very bottom of their wits to discuss by what crafty means the king may still keep Milan and draw back to him fugitive Naples, and then scheme how to conquer the Venetians, and bring under his jurisdiction all Italy, then how to win dominion over Flanders, Brabant, and all Burgundy. . . .

How, under such conditions, and among men of this sort, Hythlodaye demands, would moral exhortation be received?—how would the King and the counsellors greet his reasonable recommendation that the King mind his own business and devote himself to the domestic welfare of his own subjects? More replies—and we should be careful to distinguish the opinions of the character called More from those of the author, who wrote both sides of the dispute and may well have been ambivalent in this matter—that such advice indeed would be scorned, but he insists that the philosopher has a duty to the State, and argues that though the philosopher may not succeed in bringing about ideal conditions he may at least be able to avert the worst, may have an ameliorating effect upon the behaviour of politicians: 'If evil opinions and naughty persuasions cannot be utterly and altogether plucked out of their hearts, if you cannot, even as you would, remedy vices which habit and custom have confirmed, yet this is no cause for leaving and forsaking the commonwealth. You must not forsake the ship in a tempest, because you cannot rule and keep down the winds. . . . But you must with a crafty wile and subtle art endeavour, as much as in you lies, to handle the matter wisely and handsomely for the purpose, and that which you cannot turn to good, so order that it be not very bad.'

Viewed in retrospect, this passage seems to stand at a turning-point in the development of English humanism, and to be prophetic of what was to occur. For the arguments of Hythlodaye, by and large, were to be rejected by English humanists, and those of his opponent were to triumph. From the time of More until the breakdown of the humanist cultural hegemony in the late eighteenth century, humanist men of letters—poets, essayists, historians—were to serve the State, were to conceive of themselves in their literary aspect as public men. The pattern would be that of More, Elyot, Spenser and Milton, Swift and Bolingbroke, Pope and Burke, rather than that of Arnold's Scholar Gypsy, distant descendant of Hythlodaye and the *vagantes*.

comparing law in the State to divine reason in man's soul, and thus reaffirmed the attitude of such medieval legal philosophers as Bracton and Fortescue. Both law and reason, Starkey pointed out, are principles of order. The law of the State, based on universal natural law, represents the application of that universal law to local conditions.[24] It is upon this basis, whether made explicit or tacitly assumed, that humanist writers from Starkey to Bolingbroke differed from the alternative tradition of Machiavelli and Hobbes. For the humanists the ruler of the State was not above but under the moral law, and was a true ruler only so long as he remained so.

The moral and intellectual tradition initiated in England by such writers as these during the reign of Henry VIII survived, though not without modification, the vicissitudes of English history during the next two and a half centuries. Though some historians have argued that during the middle third of the sixteenth century humanist scholarship declined, Bush and Caspari show convincingly that this was not the case.[25] It is true that no works were produced comparable in value to those which appeared during the first thirty years of the century. Nevertheless, the task of the mid-century was to implement the programme set forth by such men as Elyot. During these middle years of the sixteenth century many new schools were founded, and old ones reorganised, and the humanist programme was made the core of their curriculum. Harrow and Rugby, Shrewsbury, Tonbridge, and the Merchant Taylors School were founded; Westminster and Canterbury were reorganised along humanist lines.[26] It was during this period, moreover, that the statesmen and men of letters of Elizabethan England received their education, and when we examine their works we find that the ethos they embody is that which the humanist pedagogues had elaborated earlier in the century. As Caspari says, the 'ideal of the learned responsible gentleman who devotes himself to the tasks of government, as envisaged by Elyot and Starkey and further elaborated by others, became the model

[24] Thomas Starkey, *A Dialogue Between Reginald Pole and Thomas Lupset*, ed. K. M. Burton (London, 1948), pp. 29–32.

[25] Caspari, pp. 132–5; Douglas Bush, 'Tudor Humanism and Henry VIII', *University of Toronto Quarterly*, VII (1938), 162–7, and also *The Renaissance and English Humanism* (Toronto, 1939), pp. 73–79.

[26] Caspari, pp. 137–43.

for an increasingly active and powerful gentry'.[27] 'Alas you wyll be ungentle Gentlemen,' George Pettie wrote in 1581, 'yf you be no schollers: you wyll doe your Prince but simple service, you wyll stande your Countrey but in slender steade, you wyll bryng yourselves but to small preferment, yf you be no Schollers.'[28] But the gentleman, nevertheless, was not to be too much the scholar, he was to avoid professionalism. His learning was to serve a practical purpose, was intended to make him a better leader and citizen than he otherwise could be. All other learning, thought Sir Thomas North, translator of Plutarch, 'is private, fitter for Universities than cities, fuller of contemplation than experience, more commendable in the students themselves than profitable unto others', and North favoured narrative as the method of moral instruction: 'stories . . . teach the living, revive the dead, so far excelling all other books, as it is better to see learning in noble men's lives, than to read it in Philosophers writings'.[29] What informed the humanist programme was thus the intention to re-emphasise the importance of the public and political realm, which they felt had been unduly neglected by preceding centuries.

During the sixteenth century the Grand Tour first became popular, initially for scholarly purposes, as a trip to the sources of humanist learning. Pole, Grocyn, Linacre, and others went to Italy to obtain instruction not available at home. But when most of the classics and the writings of the Continental humanists became available in England young gentlemen who were prospective 'governours' went abroad to acquire knowledge of foreign political conditions, of military matters, of manners and languages—the sort of knowledge, in short, that would fit them for public service. This pattern persisted into the eighteenth century as an essential part of a gentleman's training, and famous examples of it occur in the cases of Addison, Bolingbroke, Chesterfield, and Horace Walpole. Indeed, the voyage abroad for the study of other societies and cultures constituted an important theme in humanist imaginative literature from More's

[27] Ibid., p. 151.

[28] *The Civile Conversation of M. Steeven Guazzo* (London, 1581), f. I^v. Pettie translated Books I–III.

[29] Plutarch, *The Lives of the Noble Grecians and Romans*, trans. Thomas North (London, 1579), f. ii^v.

Utopia to *Gulliver's Travels*. And when Pope satirises the frivolous behaviour of a young nobleman abroad in *The Dunciad* he has it in mind to criticise his defection from an ethos which justifies the existence of his social class.[30]

It would be a simple enough matter to trace the continuity of humanist assumptions through such writers as Sidney, Spenser, Daniel, Jonson, and Milton. They all shared Spenser's aim in *The Faerie Queene*—'to fashion', as he said, 'a gentleman or noble person in virtuous and gentle discipline', and like him they considered that they were continuing the pedagogical tradition of 'all the antique Poets historicall'.[31] The strains to which the humanist tradition, with its commitment to the public world, was subjected during the seventeenth century are well known. In the realm of ideas Calvinism powerfully urged the Pauline conviction of man's sinfulness and undercut the humanist hope that his reason might be cultivated to good effect. The new science, and particularly astronomy, for a while cast doubt on the notion that nature was orderly, and thus weakened the humanist claim that nature could be viewed as exemplary, as a model of order for man's soul. The traditional social structure itself was shaken by a variety of forces, chief among them perhaps a sudden influx of wealth from overseas, which helped, by encouraging wild financial speculation, to bring about the rise of new families and the fall of old ones. The disorders of the seventeenth culminated, of course, in the Civil War, and the problems of politics were found to be amenable to the solutions of the soldier rather than of the orator. It was time, as Marvell wrote, 'to leave the Books in dust,/ And oyl th' unused Armours rust'. Nevertheless, though some of the greatest writers turned inward to seek through meditation a psychological order that had disappeared from the public world—one thinks of Donne, Herbert, Browne, Vaughan—others continued to think of themselves as orators in the humanist sense, as moralists whose duty and privilege it was to counsel and admonish the men who governed the State. Ben Jonson, as aware as Donne of the disorders of his age, remained a public moralist in his poems and plays. 'I could never', he wrote in *Timber*,

---

[30] *The Dunciad* (1743), Book IV, 11, 275–334.
[31] Edmund Spenser, *Works*, ed. J. C. Smith and E. de Selincourt (London, 1937), p. 407.

thinke the study of Wisdome confined only to the Philosopher; or of *Piety* to the *Divine*: or of *State* to the *Politicke*. But that he which can faine a Common-wealth (which is the *Poet*) can governe it with Counsels, strengthen it with Lawes, correct it with Judgements, informe it with *Religion*, and *Morals*; is all these. Wee doe not require in him meere *Elocution*; or an excellent faculty in verse; but the exact knowledge of all vertues and their Contraries; with ability to render the one lov'd, the other hated, by his proper embattling them.[32]

Jonson's works, his poems as well as his plays, describe a kind of commonwealth. Its virtuous subjects, the Sidneys, Lucy Countess of Bedford, William Camden, Sir Horace Vere, true soldiers, and poets who fulfil their function, receive the celebration they deserve; but the foolish and the wicked, the Puritans, the *nouveau riche*, the corrupt aristocracy, the financial speculators, are held up to scorn. Like Milton, who pursued Colet's humanist curriculum at St. Paul's School, Jonson intended his poetry to be doctrinal and exemplary to a nation.

The humanist tradition survived the social turmoil and Calvinist pessimism of the seventeenth century because the social conditions which had nourished humanism also survived. How little the Civil War really changed the social structure has been emphasised by recent historians: after 1660 the old families resumed their estates and their influence.[33] In fact, English society became less centralised than it had been under Elizabeth and the first two Stuarts, and resembled in important respects the society of earlier Tudor England. It is important to realise, moreover, that the country gentlemen who served as Justices of the Peace in the counties, or came down to London to sit in Parliament, or served in the administration, were not for the most part witless and sodden individuals of the Squire Western type. Often, as Plumb shows, they were men of culture and learning. The 'bulk were well educated. Their libraries, like Sir Pury Cust's or Walpole's father's, contained the classics—Homer, Thucidides, Plutarch, Livy, Cicero, Seneca, Virgil, Ovid, Lucretius, Pliny; plenty of history; Dugdale,

---

[32] *Ben Jonson*, ed. C. H. Herford, P. Simpson, E. Simpson, VIII (Oxford, 1947), p. 595.
[33] Hugh R. Trevor-Roper, 'The Social Causes of the Great Rebellion', *Men and Events* (New York, 1957), p. 204.

Brady, Holinshed, Daniel, Raleigh; some French books, perhaps, usually Bossuet, Corneille, Racine, and Bayle's Dictionary; a book or two on architecture; a great number of law books; a little poetry, Spenser and Milton, occasionally Dryden; a shelf of sermons and theology . . . At every fair in East Anglia there were bookstalls, and it was not only the local parson who bought there. Political problems were couched in historical terms. Men believed that by studying the country's past, especially its law, they could unravel the mysteries of authority and obligation which so baffled them.'[34] Men of this sort provided much of Bolingbroke's political support; their ethical assumptions were his, too, and he could count on such shared assumptions in his political writings. As this account of the books they read suggests, those assumptions were drawn from the humanist tradition. Thus the curriculum designed by Colet and More for St. Paul's persisted through the seventeenth and eighteenth centuries, and its assumptions became widely disseminated. It was this humanist curriculum that Dryden followed at Westminster, and Swift at Kilkenny, the 'Eton of Ireland', and Bolingbroke at Eton itself.

[34] J. H. Plumb, *Sir Robert Walpole*, I (Boston, 1956), p. 21.

II

BOLINGBROKE: THE PATTERN
OF A HUMANIST CAREER

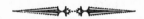

With laurels some have fatally been crown'd.

Dryden.

A POLITICAL career could hardly have been more spectacu-
lar than Bolingbroke's. Gaining the summit of political
power before he was 30, he astonished all who knew him with
his intellect and his eloquence; but a few months after holding
the destinies of nations in his hands he found himself a proscribed traitor. He spent almost a decade in exile on the
Continent. Then, through complicated manoeuvres, he was able
to return to England, and, though barred from office, again
play a leading role in political affairs. It even seemed possible,
for a time, that he might succeed in replacing Walpole as Prime
Minister, might recover the power he so suddenly had lost;
but his plans once again were frustrated, and once again he
became an exile, though a voluntary one this time, and turned
to the composition of his principal literary works.

One reason, no doubt, that Bolingbroke's career veered in
this extreme way between success and failure, office and exile,
may be found in his own nature, a strange mixture of weakness
and strength. Beyond his intimate circle he somehow failed to
inspire much trust. Men found him impressive, but they also
felt, with some reason, that his temperament was erratic, and
further, that when it suited his purposes he could be less than
candid. His occasional double-dealing cannot be excused by
observing that most other politicians of the time were guilty of

it. Even in his personal life his character showed serious flaws: he married his first wife for her money, and treated her shabbily. His exploits as a lecher were notorious. Yet despite his flaws, his accomplishments were great, and his politics essentially informed by principle. His skill as a diplomat enabled him to fashion the Peace of Utrecht under conditions of extreme difficulty; later, in his campaign against Walpole, he was fighting in actuality for the independence of Parliament, thus anticipating Burke by thirty years, and making an important contribution to the development of the British Constitution.

But if Bolingbroke's character helped to shape the course of his career, his vicissitudes also reflected the age he lived in. He was born Henry St. John on 1 October 1678 at Battersea in an old manor house that stood in a pleasant spot on the Thames, but a short trip by carriage or boat from London. Today, after two and a half centuries of progress, the neighbourhood consists of a cheap amusement park surrounded by dreary semi-slums. The year of St. John's birth also marked the peak of French power under Louis XIV, as reflected in the Treaty of Nimwegen. The power of France and the ambition of her King would be dominant factors in the political arena Bolingbroke was destined to enter. The year of Bolingbroke's birth was the year, too, in which the astonishing disclosures of Titus Oates provoked yet another crisis in an England bedeviled by political and religious discord. Nor did recent history provide assurance of stability. Only a generation before Oliver Cromwell had ruled the land by means of a military dictatorship, and in the mid-century struggle of Parliamentarian with Royalist, Puritan with Cavalier, St. John's forebears had fought on opposite sides. When St. John reached the age of 10 England had still another revolution, and another legitimate king was deposed; in 1745, six years before his death, a Jacobite army encamped at Derby and seemed likely to march on London. All of this turmoil reflected less dramatic but nontheless far-reaching changes that, as St. John came to see, were taking place in the structure of English society, in its manners and morals, in economic processes, in England's power in the world. The career of a public man in so turbulent a period could not be expected to be a serene one, especially when, penetrating in his analysis

of what was taking place, and an activist by temperament, he
refused to be passive before events.[1]

St. John's father, known as 'Old Frumps', was a man of
pleasure, distinctly, one gathers, a Restoration type. In 1864
he killed Sir William Eastcourt in a brawl at the Devil's Tavern,
but except for this his only notable accomplishment proved to
be longevity. Swift gives us a glimpse of him in November 1710,
an ageing rake who 'walks the Mall, and frequents St. James'
Coffee-house, and the Chocolate-houses', and goes on to exclaim
over the contrast between father and son: 'and the young sone
is principal secretary of state. Is there not something very odd
in that?'[2] Little love was lost between father and son. When
St. John received his title his father is supposed to have remarked
that he had always supposed his son would be hanged, but that
now he knew he would be beheaded. This may well be apoc-
ryphal, but it does suggest the quality of their relationship.
St. John's mother died while he was still a boy, and when his
father remarried, this time to a Frenchwoman, St. John was
placed under the supervision of his grandmother Joanna,
daughter of Oliver St. John, the great Puritan lawyer. In his
later years he was a good deal less than grateful for the pains she
had taken with him, and was accustomed to refer to this period
of his life with disgust. One of the theologians whose voluminous
works filled her library, he recalled, was the Presbyterian
divine Dr. Manton, who prided himself on having written a
hundred and nineteen sermons on the hundred and nineteenth
Psalm, and she obliged him to spend long hours with these
edifying discourses. Many years later he wrote to Swift of Dr.
Manton as the one 'who taught my youth to yawn, and prepared me to be a High-Churchman, that I might never hear
him read, nor read him more'.[3] Eventually, young St. John
escaped from the severity of Joanna's supervision by entering Eton.

[1] See Sir Charles Petrie, *Bolingbroke* (London, 1937), pp. 13–14. Also useful in
the preparation of this chapter and the two following have been J. Churton
Collins, *Bolingbroke* (London, 1886), J. H. Plumb, *The First Four Georges* (London,
1956), and *Sir Robert Walpole*, 2 vols. (Boston, 1956–61), Walter Sichel, *Bolingbroke
and His Times*, 2 vols. (London, 1901–2). All of the books on Bolingbroke, however,
need to be corrected in the light of more recent information and points of view,
especially in regard to the relationship between Bolingbroke's life and his works.
[2] *Journal to Stella*, ed. Sir Harold Williams, I (Oxford, 1948), 92.
[3] *The Correspondence of Jonathan Swift*, ed. F. Elrington Ball, III (London, 1914),
p. 93.

Details concerning his school years are regrettably scarce. We do know from a letter he wrote to his sister Henrietta in 1717 that he had experienced some difficulty in adjusting himself to the Eton programme:

> Your sending the eldest of your two sons to Eton makes me hope that his health is mended. It is late for him to go thither unless he has been instructed according to the method of that school. I remember the pain it cost me to fall into that method, and to overtake those in points of form who were behind me in knowledge of the Latin tongue.[4]

Other phrases in the letter no doubt reflect his memories of his own Eton days. The boy will need 'a good deal of spirit and ambition to get forward', he tells his sister, and he also hopes that she will 'keep him there till he is confirmed in the Latin at least. Some of the best books in the world have been written in that language . . .'[5] The letter suggests that fierce ambition and love of the classics were prominent among his characteristics at Eton, as in later life. Robert Walpole was there at the same time, and Horace Walpole remarks that as early as their school years 'they had set out rivals'.[6] We may easily suppose that their rivalry then exhibited the same contrasts that it did later: St. John lively, high-strung, brilliant, Walpole solid and plodding, working hard for every success.

A doubtful tradition exists that St. John passed on from Eton to Oxford and impressed the dons there with his extraordinary abilities, but there is no certainty that he did go to Oxford, and, if he did, it was not for long, since no record of him as a student remains there. What is beyond doubt, however, is that in one way or another, whether at Eton, or reading on his own, he acquired a first-rate education. Based solidly upon classical history and literature, it was precisely the sort of education the humanists of the Renaissance had designed for the statesman. What St. John had accomplished by 1697, when he was 19, we know from a series of remarkable letters he wrote to Sir William Trumbull from the Continent. Liberal learning had not, surely, made him as virtuous in his private life as men like

[4] Letter dated 24 July, 1717, British Museum MSS. 34196.
[5] Ibid.
[6] Horace Walpole, *Memoirs of the Last Ten Years of the Reign of George the Second*, I (London, 1822), p. 195.

More and Erasmus would have hoped, but it had prepared him to survey the nations of Europe with a discerning eye as he completed his prepartion for a diplomatic career. None of St. John's biographers has discerned the importance of his relationship to Trumbull. As we read these letters, however, it seems clear that Trumbull provided for him an example of the sort of person he wished to be. St. John's own father was ignorant, a failure, and indifferent to his son. Trumbull was in every way the opposite.

In 1697, then, St. John took advantage of the pause in hostilities brought about by the Treaty of Ryswick and left for the Continent, where he was to spend almost two years. At 19 we may suppose him to have appeared much as he did at the peak of his career a few years later. He was tall, aquilinely handsome, and had a dark complexion, and though there was something nervously taut about him, this was most often concealed by his elegantly formal manner. His urbanity, remarkable even in the eighteenth century, was destined to inspire a proverb. 'To make St. John more polite' became a synonym for useless labour, like carrying coals to Newcastle. 'Lord Bolingbroke,' said Aaron Hill, 'was the finest gentleman I ever saw.'[7] Travelling first to Paris, St. John then moved on to Geneva, and there spent the summer of 1698 studying Civil Law. A letter he wrote to Trumbull from Geneva in July contains an especially striking passage—striking because so suddenly personal in the midst of his lengthy accounts of political and economic conditions—which sheds a good deal of light on his relationship to the older man. 'Having chose you for my pattern,' he writes, 'and being resolved to draw as good a copy as I can after so excellent an original, I apply myself to that study in which you became so perfect a master; and tho' I despair of arriving to the same pitch I am resolved it shall be my misfortune and not my fault.'[8] The study he refers to here was the law, in which Trumbull had achieved pre-eminence. Yet in this passage St. John implies that he intends more than an imitation of Trumbull's legal skill. He has chosen Trumbull for his pattern, he says, and

[7] J. H. Plumb, *Sir Robert Walpole*, I, p. 130. J. Churton Collins, *Bolingbroke*, p. 8.

[8] H. M. C. Downshire MSS., Vol. I, Pt. 2, p. 782, quoted in Petrie, *Bolingbroke*, p. 21.

throughout the correspondence, as he reports to Trumbull his reflections upon what he has seen in his travels, as he parades his erudition and alludes to his ambitions, Trumbull plays for him the role of guide, philosopher, and friend.

The passage of time since that summer of 1698 has reversed the order of magnitude between the two men, Trumbull and St. John. Trumbull has been forgotten by all except scholars, while his young friend, as a politician, as a political theorist, as an influence upon Pope, remains at least on the periphery of our awareness. But in 1698 Trumbull had recently retired as Secretary of State, and was an illustrious figure to all who were aware of events in the public world. Not only had he been an important statesman and diplomat, he was also a man of liberal learning, of superior tastes and wide cultivation, the companion of poets and men of letters. Dryden, it will be remembered, remarks in the postscript to his translation of Virgil that 'if the last Aeneid shine amongst its fellows, it is owing to the commands of Sir William Trumbull . . . who recommended it to my care'.[9] A few years later Trumbull gave another and younger poet the benefit of his advice. About 1705 Trumbull made the acquaintance of Alexander Pope, and they soon developed the habit of riding together almost daily, and, as Pope later told Spence, they had long conversations on their common enthusiasm, classical literature.[10] When Pope, then 16, showed Trumbull his translation of the 'Epistle of Sarpedon from the twelfth and sixteenth book of the Iliad', Trumbull urged him to translate the whole epic, which of course he later did, recalling to Trumbull in a letter written in November 1713, 'your opinion and Judgment, which has at last moved me to undertake the translation of Homer. I can honestly say, Sir William Trumbull was not only the first that put this into my Thoughts, but the principal encourager I had in it . . .'[11] Indeed, on the basis of the recently discovered Pope-Trumbull correspondence, George Sherburn concludes that Trumbull must have been Pope's most important adviser during these earliest years of his career as a poet. Pope read his Pastorals to

[9] *The Poetical Works of Dryden*, ed. G. R. Noyes (Cambridge, 1950), p. 708.
[10] George Sherburn, 'Letters of Alexander Pope, Chiefly to Sir William Trumbull', RES, IX (1958), 389.
[11] Ibid.

Trumbull, and dedicated *Spring* to him, and he devoted a long passage in *Windsor Forest* to praising Trumbull's withdrawal to a life of contemplative retirement.[12] Both Pope and St. John thus knew Trumbull after he had retired from public life to spend his last years in study and reflection. Such retirement, of course, completed a pattern familiar in classical treatises on ethics, and there was, indeed, something self-consciously 'classical' about the tone of Trumbull's retirement. Then, too, Trumbull's life of gardening and conversation, literature and philosophy, must have been all the more striking for the contrast it provided to his earlier years, when he had served the State as diplomat, Member of Parliament, and Secretary of State.

'Having chose you for my pattern,' wrote St. John from Geneva, 'and being resolved to draw as good a copy as I can after so excellent an original'—and we can see, I think, what he meant. St. John intended to emulate the pattern implicit in his education and examplified by Trumbull, the pattern set forth by humanist theoreticians, and which combined public service with learning, chiefly classical, and a broad concern with letters, because literature was a principal source of public virtue. When St. John travelled on the Continent in 1697 he was repeating an experience Trumbull himself had enjoyed, as had countless other representatives of this social and cultural tradition, for such a Grand Tour was understood to be the final stage of a young man's preparation for the career of a statesman.

St. John's letters to Trumbull are in the nature of reports on his tour, and it is evident that he wrote them with the intention of gaining the older man's approval. Throughout this correspondence, moreover, we find, already formed, the attitudes which would always be central to his mind. First of all, there is his abhorrence of arbitrary power. This was to be elaborated upon in his critique of Machiavelli in *The Idea of a Patriot King*. Then, too, it is evident that his usable past, the standard he uses to judge what he sees, is ancient Rome, a perfectly natural preference for one brought up in the humanist tradition. 'There is nothing I think that contributes more to the Roman glory than their law,' he writes to Trumbull, and he considers that Roman law remained a powerful force for civilization even after 'their state was confounded by the northern rabble of

---

[12] See *Windsor Forest*, 11, 235–58.

Huns, Goths, and Vandals'. Furthermore, and this is particularly important, he identifies Roman law with what he would afterwards call the 'spirit of patriotism', by which he meant a disinterested commitment to public order. There was a time in England, he writes, when Roman law prevailed, 'when their divine spirit (if I may use the expression) shed its influence on us; there was a time when *dulce et decorum est pro patria mori* was imprinted on our hearts'. No doubt there is a good deal of attitudinising in all this; like his contemporaries, St. John liked to don the toga; but there is in it, as well, a genuine devotion to the idea of public service, a willingness to accept the responsibilities of a member of the governing class.

Touring in a leisurely fashion, he travelled from Geneva to Turin to Milan, and reached Rome by May 1699. Trumbull had written to him about the condition of learning at Rome, observing that it 'it is not at a very low ebb there, and must be so where the Priests and their Inquisition govern'. Nevertheless, he had asked St. John to enquire about the edition of the New Testament that one Alexander Zacagnius reportedly was preparing, and also to look into the activities of the famous Della Cruscan Academy at Florence. St. John's reply of 13 May exhibits some of the characteristic humanist attitudes. He reports that two cardinals at Rome, the most learned men to be found there, have written many books, but that most of these books are 'all scholastic learning and so much out of my way that I have not yet looked into any'. He also tells Trumbull about some other books, 'little scraps' of 'History and Chronology which I design to buy', and, in this case, praises in humanist fashion their 'pure and elegant style'.

Akin to his contempt for scholasticism and his admiration for a pure and elegant style was his dislike for pedantry. Sometimes, indeed, there is a pedantic quality in his avoidance of it: one senses that he will write 'I think Tacitus tells us . . .' even when he knows very well that Tacitus has done so. In June he wrote to Trumbull from Leghorn, giving an account of his trip to Tuscany. 'Before my coming to Florence I had heard talk of Magliabecchi (Antonio), Library Keeper to the great Duke, as one of the most . . . learned men of this age; nay, even in Graevius and Cardinal Neris's works I had here and there found the greatest commendations imaginable of him. . . .

Upon my arrival here he was the first man I sought, but . . . I found an old, vain, senseless pedant, a great devourer of books without any method or judgment to digest what he reads, a kind of Bethlem character, one that is always busy without proposing to himself an end. . . .' In St. John's description Magliabecchi might be a character from the sixteenth-century *Epistolae obscurorum virorum*, or from Pope's *Dunciad*, or one of those whose useless erudition Erasmus and Rabelais had satirised. The same attitudes informed St. John's judgments.

He was far, however, from confining himself to broad attitudes and easy judgments on his tour of the Continent. As humanist educators had always recommended, he paid close attention to the details of foreign cultures and Governments, cataloguing his observations for Trumbull with an assiduity he would later show in his performance as a statesman. He made careful notes on political conditions, and studied 'the secret springs which turn and move' the policies of Courts. He perfected his knowledge of foreign tongues, becoming so proficient that he would later seem something of a foreigner to more insular Englishmen. Yet if he did not waste his time on the Continent, he did, perhaps, in some ways resemble that young nobleman who, according to Pope, 'intrigue'd with glory, and with spirit whor'd' while travelling in Europe. Years later he was to write to the Earl of Essex a letter in which he recalls his own experiences abroad:

> . . . I make my compliments to Captain Feilding on the jolly night he passed with his country men. But I have some faint remembrance that I used, in every country where he is, to pass my nights more silently and yet more rapturously.[13]

From his letters to Trumbull it seems evident that the old statesman played a part in St. John's development rather like that of Sir William Temple in Swift's. One need not agree with the conclusion of Irvin Ehrenpries that Temple was the model for the King of Brobdinghag in order to acknowledge the validity of Middleton Murry's opinion, based upon a close analysis of Swift's verse, that Temple embodied for Swift the traditional humanist ideal, the wise man who plays a responsible part in the affairs of the State, and whose wisdom and

[13] British Museum MSS. 27732, dated 1 October 1732.

virtue derive from his study of the classics. Perhaps, as Middleton Murry puts it, the orphaned Swift sought a father in Temple. And St. John, though not exactly fatherless, may well have recognised in Trumbull a model commensurate with his intelligence and ambition, such a model as his own father could scarcely provide.[14]

Returning to England in 1700, St. John attracted less attention with his intelligence and seriousness than through his talents as a libertine. Goldsmith tells the story of St. John and his friends running naked across St. James's Park, and he is supposed to have made his relative Rochester his model in exploits such as this. Whether or not this legend is true, there is no doubt that he drank hard, particularly champagne and burgundy, and was flamboyant in his pursuit of women. In his letters to his friend Thomas Cook, M.P. for Derbyshire, there are such casual remarks as these: 'Really, Tom, you are missed: whoring flags without you.' He kept one Miss Gumley, a fashionable whore, and wrote verses to a certain Clara who sold oranges in the lobby of the Court of Requests ('Be to thy Harry ever kind and true,/ And live for him who more than dies for you'), and he was generally supposed to have cuckholded one Brigadier Breton.[15] Even the duties of high office seem to have distracted him little from these activities. 'Lord Radnor and I', wrote Swift a few years later, 'were walking in the Mall this evening; and Mr. Secretary met us, took a turn or two, and then stole away, and we both believed it was to pick up a wench.'

In May of 1701 he married Frances Winchcombe, daughter of a considerable landowner in Berkshire. His treatment of her was disgraceful, even though she, for her part, loved him deeply and remined loyal to him despite his famous debauches. It seems that he married her for her money; he habitually spent far beyond his means, and no doubt the £3,000 this marriage added to his annual income was more than welcome. 'That I was married last Thursday is a trifling piece of news,' he wrote to Sir William Trumbull, and the tone of this remark suggests

---

[14] See Irwin Ehrenpreis, 'Gulliver', *The Personality of Jonathan Swift* (London, 1958), pp. 83–116; also John Middleton Murry, *Jonathan Swift* (New York, 1955), Ch. II.

[15] Petrie, *Bolingbroke*, p. 31.

quite accurately what his attitude towards his marriage must have been. His thoughts in 1701, moreover, were no doubt political rather than matrimonial, for that year he commenced the public career for which he had so long and so thoroughly prepared, becoming Member of Parliament for Wootton Basset, a family borough in Wiltshire.

Accounts of St. John's career between 1701 and 1715 have dwelt upon many things—the brilliance of his maiden speech, his enormous capacity for work when in office, first as Secretary of War under the Godolphin ministry, then as Secretary of State in Harley's ministry—but his consistency of political principle has gone unrecognised. As St. John himself observes, 'the part which I acted . . . in the first essays I made in public affairs, was the part of a tory, and so far of a piece with that which I acted afterwards' (i.e. until 1715).[16] He is careful to explain what he means by Tory:

> We looked on the political principles which had generally prevailed in our government from the revolution in one thousand six hundred and eighty-eight to be destructive of our true interest, to have mingled us too much in the affairs of the continent, to tend to the impoverishing of our people, and to the loosening the bands of our constitution in church and state. We supposed the tory party to be the bulk of the landed interest, and to have no contrary influence blended into its composition. We supposed the Whigs to be the remains of a party formed against the ill designs of a court under king Charles the Second, nursed up into strength and applied to contrary uses by king William the Third, and yet still so weak as to lean for support on the presbyterians and other sectaries, on the bank and the other corporations, on the Dutch and the other allies.[17]

When he later affirms the principles of the Revolution of 1688 with respect to the monarchy he does not contradict this earlier attitude, for in speaking here of the 'political principles which had prevailed' since the Revolution, he does not mean the constitutional principles but rather the growing power of what he calls 'the moneyed interest'. His concern as a Minister, and as a political polemicist after he had been denied the right of holding office, was to prevent the moneyed interest from in-

[16] *The Works of Lord Bolingbroke*, I (Philadelphia, 1841), p. 114.
[17] Ibid., I, p. 115.

fluencing the Government to the detriment of other interests in the community. He sets forth his position with great precision:

> The bank, the East India company, and in general the moneyed interest, had certainly nothing to apprehend like what they feared, or affected to fear from the tories, an entire subversion of their property. Multitudes of our own party would have been wounded by such a blow. The intention of those, who were the warmest, seemed to me to go no farther than restraining their influences on the legislature . . . that which touched sensibly even those who were but little moved by other considerations was the prodigious inequality between the condition of the moneyed men and of the rest of the nation.[18]

St. John thus conceived of the 'moneyed interest' as but one part of the community, and he intended to prevent it from abusing its growing power at the expense of the rest of the nation. He thought, moreover, that the proper working of the Constitution depended upon the independence of Parliament, and by independence he meant its freedom from domination by any single 'interest' or 'faction' in the nation. Before 1715 he considered the power of the moneyed interest to be the main threat to the Constitution, and he viewed both the Crown and an independent Parliament as instruments for controlling it. After 1715 he thought that the Crown itself had been captured by this 'faction', and that the independence of Parliament had been undermined by Walpole's methods, and he therefore launched a furious campaign on behalf of an independent Parliament. From the start, accordingly, the middle and smaller landowners constituted the basis of his political strength. The large landowners could diversify their investments and dabble in commerce, but the lesser owners faced the problems created by the fact that their incomes were limited in source and amount

---

[18] Ibid., I, p. 116. He makes the same point elsewhere; cf. *On the Study of Use of History*: 'When you look back three or four generations ago, you will see that the English were a plain, perhaps a rough, but a good natured hospitable people, jealous of their liberties, and able as well as ready to defend them, with their tongues, their pens, and their swords. . . . Since the revolution, our kings have been reduced indeed to a seeming annual dependence on Parliament; but the business of parliament, which was esteemed in general a duty before, has been exercised in general as a trade since. The trade of parliament, and the trade of funds, have grown universal.' (*Bolingbroke*, II, pp. 332–3.)

at a time when prices were rising and the burdens of taxation heavier. As the century went on the gap between the country squires and the small landowners on the one hand and the great landowners and investors on the other tended to widen, for the small owner had too little room for manoeuvre.[19] It was from this class that St. John drew his most consistent support. Their grievances found expression in the October Club, and, later on, made them receptive to the *Craftsman*'s polemic. As Swift put it in the *Examiner* early in the reign of Queen Anne:

> Let any man observe the Equipages in this Town; he shall find the greater Number of those who make a Figure, to be of a Speciaes of Men quite different from any that were ever known before the Revolution; consisting either of Generals and Colonels, or of such whose whole fortunes lie in Funds and Stocks: so that *Power*, which according to the old Maxim, was used to follow *Land*, is now gone over to Money.[20]

From the start of his political career St. John made an enormous impression on his associates, and he quickly became a leader in the House. In 1704 the Whiggish Godolphin ministry made him Secretary-at-War in an attempt to quiet its Parliamentary critics, and his performance in this post was admired even by those who detested his politics. During these years of Marlborough's successful campaigns and great early victories St. John often worked at his desk from ten in the morning until eight at night, never relaxing into carelessness of detail, and he was famous for his ability to put in a full day of this sort after a night of champagne drinking.

When he could spare the time he repaired to Bucklebury, a property near Reading which he had acquired through his marriage.[21] In his *Journal to Stella*, Swift describes the kind of life St. John liked to lead in the country: 'Mr. Secretary was a perfect country gentleman at Bucklebury; he smoked tobacco with one or two neighbours; he inquired after the wheat in such a field; he went to visit his hounds, and knew all their names; he and his lady saw me to my chamber just in the

[19] G. E. Mingay, *English Landed Society in the Eighteenth Century* (London, 1963), pp. 85, 216.

[20] Jonathan Swift, *Examiner*, ed. Herbert Davis (Oxford, 1957), p. 5.

[21] Godfrey Davies and Marion Tinling, 'Letters of Henry St. John to James Brydges', *Huntingdon Library Bulletin*, IX (1935), pp. 153-70.

country fashion.'[22] St. John's attachment to the country undoubtedly was sincere, and this may have been one quality
that, as Petrie remarks, enabled him to hold the allegiance of
country gentlemen who resembled him in little else. As Secretary at War he worked closely with Marlborough, and their
relations, soon to be so embittered, were amicable. An amusing
anecdote depicts them together at the War Office. Joshua
Barnes, Professor of Greek at Cambridge, brought to the War
Office an edition of Anacreon, which he expected to dedicate
to Marlborough in the hope of financial reward. 'Mr St. John,
who was Secretary-at-War, was then in the room, and the Duke
comes up to him: "Dear Harry, here's a man comes to me and
talks to me about one Anna Creon, and I know nothing of
Creon, but Creon in the play of Oedipus, prithee do you speak
to the man." Mr. St. John said the Duke never gave the man
any, but he was himself forced to pay him.'[23] Marlborough's
miserliness contrasts comically with his military genius, but the
war itself was anything but comic. The gentry groaned under
the land tax, which was the principal source of Government
revenue, and grew embittered over the fortunes being made by
speculation in London. And the records of St. John's Secretary-
ship contain moving glimpses of the suffering of some who had
fought across the Channel. On 3 July 1704, for example, he
submitted a proposal to relieve 'maimed soldiers and marines
who, being dismissed from her Majesties service abroad, come
over in great numbers to Harwich', and he requested a fund
to pay their way home from Harwich, for 'they often had to
beg, or died of disease in that town'.[24]

In 1706 the Allied cause prospered spectacularly. Marlborough's astonishing victory at Blenheim had saved Austria,
Ramilies had cleared the French out of the Spanish Netherlands, Prince Eugène had routed the French before Turin, and
Galway had been able to go over to the offensive in Spain.
Under these circumstances the avowed war aims of the Allies
could certainly have been achieved had they been willing to
negotiate a peace, but instead the war dragged on, causing, as
its weeks became months and then years, increasing resentment

[22] *Journal to Stella*, 4 and 5 August 1711.
[23] G. M. Trevelyan, *Ramilies*, Vol. II of *The Age of Queen Anne* (London, 1938), p. 8.
[24] British Museum MSS. 28948.

over the policies of the administration.[25] St. John resigned as Secretary-at-War in 1707, sensing the growing vulnerability of the Whig ministry, and decided not to stand for re-election in 1708, choosing rather to spend that year repairing his political fences and waiting for the opportunity to put his own principles into effect in a Tory ministry.

This turned out to be a wise move, for everywhere, by the end of 1708, Whig policies were at a disadvantage. The Queen had never liked the Whigs. Though a Protestant, she was the daughter of James II, and religious orthodoxy had always been close to her heart. She did not trust the Whigs, who seemed more concerned than they ought to have been with the well-being of the Dissenters, and with commercial profits. Indeed, popular dislike of the Dissenters once again was inflamed. The Naturalisation Act had enabled a horde of impoverished, Calvinistic aliens to cross into England from the Continent, and many thought that the Whigs had brought them in to subvert the Church. They seemed unassimilable; they also put Englishmen out of work. To make matters worse, peace conferences at Gertruydensberg had failed and the end of the war seemed as distant as ever, as did the end of the taxes the war made necessary. The ministry sensed that it needed a flamboyant stroke to revive its waning fortunes, and so, in an attempt to disgrace its critics, it impeached the arch-Tory Sacheverell for a violent sermon he had preached against the Government. Sacheverell's trial only intensified resentment against the Whigs, and provided Anne with a long-awaited opportunity to dismiss her Ministers.[26] On the eighth of August, Godolphin received a curt note from the Queen telling him that his services were no longer required, and that instead of bringing her his White Staff he should simply break it. Understandably exasperated by such treatment, Godolphin broke the staff and threw it into his fireplace. Whig gloom could scarcely have been deeper. Henry Watkins wrote to Horatio Walpole from Berlin that 'I can scarce hold up my head under the heavy burden of the news we have received this day from England. Our comfort is that we have not our hopes in this world . . .'[27] Other correspon-

---

[25] Petrie, *Bolingbroke*, p. 91; Plumb, *Sir Robert Walpole*, I, pp. 127–8.
[26] Plumb, *Sir Robert Walpole*, I, pp. 143–6; Collins, *Bolingbroke*, pp. 52–55.
[27] British Museum MSS. 38501.

dents were driven to financial, not religious, reflections on the fall of the Whigs. The connection of the Whig cause with the moneyed interest emerges clearly in another letter Horatio received from Berlin: 'Yesterday we had the news of my Ld. Treasurer breaking his staff . . . People here are uneasy for the money they have in the funds, but few think of withdrawing it till they hear what is done in the peace, which is expected soon . . . The Prince Royal[28] is a keen Whig and called the Torys rogues, etc.'[29]

At the Queen's command Robert Harley began to form a ministry, attempting in his characteristic fashion to trim between the two parties, evidently wishing to avoid complete dependence on the Tories. He even had conferences with Cowper, Halifax, and Walpole, telling them that 'there was a Whig game intended at bottom'. When asked what he meant he became unintelligible. The leading Whigs declined his offers, and it soon became clear that a coalition ministry was out of the question. Rochester accordingly succeeded Somers as President of the Council, and St. John received the Seals as Secretary of State for the Northern Department. In the general election that took place in September the decision was almost universally in favour of the Tories. Bells clanged joyously from the Tory strongholds, and by night bonfires raged in the squares. Mobs wild with excitement demolished Dissenting meeting-houses, and some of the outlying towns looked as if they had been exposed to the depredations of an invading army. 'Your Majesty,' said the Duke of Beaufort to Anne, 'is now Queen indeed.'[30]

The star of St. John now rose rapidly into the ascendant, for the all-important task was ending the war. 'A peace must be had,' as the Earl of Orrery wrote to St. John, 'and all mankind sees plainly now in how vile a manner former opportunities were neglected of making better than at this hour we have reason to expect.'[31] The peace was the hinge on which all turned. Once that was achieved, other Tory prospects would open. If

[28] Of Prussia.
[29] Mr. Cunningham to Horatio Walpole, 30 August 1710. British Museum MSS. 38, 501.
[30] The foregoing account follows Collins, *Bolingbroke*, pp. 53–56; Petrie, *Bolingbroke*, pp. 113–21, and Plumb, *Sir Robert Walpole*, I, pp. 130–62.
[31] To St. John, 30 March 1711; British Museum MSS. 37209.

the Queen lived, the Tories might entrench themselves so strongly in power that they would be irremovable when she died, or the Pretender might be won over to the Anglican Church and a Stuart succession assured. St. John was well suited to the diplomatic task. He had profited greatly from his tour of the Continent ten years before; his mastery of French and his cosmopolitan ease facilitated his negotiations with the Marquis de Torcy, the nephew of Colbert, who was the French Foreign Minister, and he had, in addition, a firm grasp of the problems of European politics. He was also sensitive to the importance of public opinion, and took care to enlist the most able writers he could find in the Tory cause. Swift helped to prepare public opinion for the peace with attacks on Marlborough in the *Examiner* and with his powerful indictment of the Dutch, *The Conduct of the Allies*. Matthew Prior, who was as polished a diplomat as he was a versifier, conducted the preliminary negotiations with the French. Swift's account of these months when the groundwork for the peace was being laid suggests something of the excitement that pervaded Tory circles. On one occasion, for instance, Swift attended a secret meeting between Prior and St. John and some French emissaries:

> I came here a day sooner than ordinary, at Mr. Secretary's desire, and supped with him and Prior, and two private ministers from France, and a French priest. I know not the two ministers names; but they are come about the Peace. The names the secretary called them, I suppose, were feigned; they were good rational men. We have already settled all things with France, and very much to the honour and advantage of England; and the Queen is in mighty good humour . . . The French ministers staid with us till one, and the secretary and I sat up talking till two.[32]

The negotiations also involved months of difficult and detailed bargaining, the progress of which can be traced in St. John's correspondence with Torcy. A sense of great urgency pervades the letters on both sides: 'We are in the most critical situation Europe has been in for many years,' writes St. John on 21 May 1712, 'and the answer I shall receive to these despatches will

[32] G. M. Trevelyan, *The Peace and the Protestant Succession* (London, 1934), p. 182.

either make peace certain or plunge us into the misfortunes of war.'[33] Each statesman knew the magnitude of the other's need for peace, and Torcy skilfully used St. John's need as a lever, but St. John was at least his equal as a negotiator. It was 'Greek meet Greek,' observes G. M. Trevelyan, 'and blade cut blade'.[34] St. John had to admit to Torcy that 'you'll see our Parliament, which is going to meet, as much disposed to Peace, as it has ever been to war'. But he could also use pressure: 'You have often repeated it to me, Sir, that there is no time to be lost. I agree with you, Sir, in that. But we do lose time, and we shall lose it; till we settle this point, our plenipotentiaries at Utrecht will remain idle.'[35] The surprising thing is that the two antagonists not only respected each other's skill but became close friends, and this, too, is part of the drama of their letters.

But if St. John faced a resourceful and highly professional opponent in Torcy, he also had to deal with powerful interests at home. The Board of Trade insisted that the French could not be allowed to fish off Newfoundland, or 'the good of our having Newfoundland restored to us will be defeated'.[36] The Dutch were reported to be 'hatching intrigues' with 'the factions in both Houses', hoping to upset the negotiations.[37] By pressing forward with the peace, moreover, he was alienating the Tories from the Elector of Hanover, a fateful but inevitable consequence of Tory policy. 'I am sorry to hear, but not surprised,' he wrote to Thomas Harley, Ambassador at Hanover,

> that the Elector's answers, when he condescends to give any, concerning peace, are such as his minister used to honour me with. It is to be hoped that he will not long resist that conviction which the truth you do not fail to tell him carries along with it. But be that as it will, her majesty pursues, and will continue to pursue the true interest, so long neglected, and even sacrificed, of her kingdom in the first place, and that of her allies, as far forth as they will suffer her to do it, in the second.[38]

[33] British Museum MSS. 49971, dated 21 May 1712.
[34] G. M. Trevelyan, ed., *Bolingbroke's Defence of the Treaty of Utrecht* (Cambridge, 1932); see introduction.
[35] British Museum MSS. 49971, dated 25 November 1711 and 21 July 1712.
[36] British Museum MSS. 35913.
[37] British Museum MSS. 41971.
[38] British Museum MSS. 34196, dated 23 July 1712.

At the beginning of August 1712 St. John went to Paris to conclude the peace. Three weeks before he had been elevated to the peerage, and henceforth would be Viscount Bolingbroke, a reward for his efforts on behalf of the treaty, but a disappointment in that he had hoped for an earldom. Nevertheless, his trip to Paris was the climax of his public career. The journey inland from Calais resembled a royal progress, and everywhere he went in France he met with adulation. He was received by Louis XIV at Fontainebleau, and when he went to the theatre to see a production of Corneille's *Le Cid*, the entire house rose in his honour, and the performance halted until he had taken his seat. He acquired, incidentally, as his latest mistress an ex-nun named Claudine de Tencin. Receiving the adulation of a nation beaten and impoverished in a long war, he must indeed have seemed as Pope put it, 'the greatest man in the world'.

The fury of the Whigs over the signing of the treaty was all the more intense because it was impotent. 'The clamour which the Whigs raise', wrote the Earl of Strafford to Bolingbroke, 'and the rage which they express are almost without example.'[39] And when the Whigs returned to power their first concern was the prosecution for treason of those responsible for ending the war. The collapse of the Tories after the death of Anne has tended to obscure the magnitude of Bolingbroke's achievement, yet most historians agree that, despite the outcries of the Whigs, the Treaty of Utrecht was a triumph of English policy, and that in bringing it about Bolingbroke exhibited high skills as a statesman and political analyst. 'Bolingbroke', writes J. H. Plumb, 'knew how the public at large hated the endless war', and he succeeded in ending it 'against the violent opposition of many of the ablest and most powerful men in politics'. His support came from the independents and rural Tories 'who represented truly enough the feelings of the nation at large', and cared little for the desire of London merchants that France be crushed for ever.[40] Bolingbroke later defended his policy with great care in Letters VI through VIII of *On the Study and Use of History*, and in these arguments Bolingbroke, writes G. M. Trevelyan, 'has, in my opinion, completely made out

[39] British Museum MSS. 49970, dated 13 February 1713.
[40] J. H. Plumb, *Sir Robert Walpole*, I, pp. 185–6.

his case', as well as exhibiting formidable powers of political analysis. The first part of Letter VI shows 'the acute and powerful mind of the author generalizing on the causes and character of the Reformation and the rise of national monarchies with an insight that even at this day is suggestive and illuminating',[41] and the other letters go on to examine the background and meaning of Utrecht. Deeply impressed with the threat posed to England by the rise of French power in the seventeenth century, Bolingbroke blames Cromwell for not seeing this, and also criticizes the pro-French policies of Charles II. Bolingbroke's hero is William III, who resisted France, but was moderate in his aims, and he argues that Utrecht represented a triumph for a Williamite policy carried out under Tory auspices. Marlborough and the Whigs, like the Emperor of Lilliput, erred in the unlimited character of their aims; by insisting that the Austrian Charles be King of Spain they would in effect have united Spain and Austria and thereby have upset the balance of power. And he justifies the deception used by the Tories in negotiating the treaty as made necessary by the impossible position of Marlborough and the Whigs.[42]

But the concluding of the peace did not bring to an end, as Bolingbroke had hoped, the problems of the Tories. Rather, it made them insoluble. He returned from his triumphs to find the ministry surrounded by problems and beset with internal divisions. Parliament threw out the Commercial Treaty on which Bolingbroke had particularly prided himself, and the malt tax moved the Scottish Members into the ranks of the Opposition. Argyle feuded openly with Harley, with whom Bolingbroke by now was scarcely on speaking terms. The Queen, to make matters worse, was in obvious decline: 'a huge, moribund bulk of a woman, she was rotting away in Kensington Palace, obstinate, indecisive, in terror of death'.[43] Bolingbroke's dilemma was compounded by the fact that the heir to the throne, the Elector of Hanover, had been an ardent supporter of the war. 'I must tell you,' George had informed Thomas Harley in 1712, 'I cannot depart from what I take to be the

---

[41] *Bolingbroke's Defence of the Treaty of Utrecht;* see introduction by G. M. Trevelyan.
[42] Ibid.
[43] J. H. Plumb, *Sir Robert Walpole,* I, p. 186.

true best interest of the Empire and the Dutch.'[44] Bolingbroke knew that when he became King, and his succession seemed imminent, he would in effect be a Whig King. The only alternative to George was the son of James II, known to Protestants as the Pretender, who had set up his Court at St. Germains. His chances of coming to power were difficult to calculate, but they would be much improved if he could be persuaded to renounce Catholicism and turn Protestant. In that case the Act of Succession might be set aside and a Whiggish régime forestalled. But the deeper the emergency grew, and the more imminent seemed the Whig wrath, the more dilatory and irresolute became Harley. Apparently caring for little besides the aggrandisement of his family, and having, indeed, many Whig sympathies, he could seldom be prevailed upon to discuss public affairs, and when he actually did so it was impossible to tell what he meant. He sank for extended periods into alcoholic reverie, and he was frequently not available when he was needed at the centre of affairs. Occasionally ill health was his excuse; most of the time he made no excuse at all.

Still, even as Tory prospects darkened and he manoeuvred to replace Harley as leading minister, Bolingbroke was not entirely occupied with matters of high politics. One previously unknown incident from these months, a very moving one, and shedding a good deal of light on the condition of English Catholics at the time, can be reconstructed from his correspondence with Prior and Torcy from December through March 1713/14. Young Henry Villiers, second son of the first Earl of Jersey and a cousin of Bolingbroke's, had been spirited away to France by his mother to be raised as a Roman Catholic. Bolingbroke himself was a cosmopolitan deist, and it is difficult to imagine that it made much difference to him whether the boy became a Catholic or not, and the strong terms of the letter he wrote to him in December 1713 probably reflect the feelings of the boy's relatives in England.

Dear Kinsman:
    The very dangerous situation in which you are at present, the relation I have to you, and the sincere love I have for you, constrain me to write this letter, which I hope will come safe

[44] B. Curtis Brown, *The Letters of Queen Anne* (London, 1935), p. 372.

to your hands. Your present, your future, your eternal happiness or misery depend on the resolutions you will now take. If you continue any longer with your mother you must bid adieu to your family and your friends, to your country and religion. You must forfeit all that is dear and renounce all that is sacred. For whatever she may pretend to make you, her true design is to make you a Papist. If on the other hand you have virtue and grace enough, as I persuade myself you have, to know that, as you owe something to your mother, so you owe something to yourself, and infinitely more than both to God.[45]

Bolingbroke was far from relying only upon persuasion to effect young Villiers's return. Soon he was writing to Prior in Paris:

I agree that the most eligible way of getting my cousin Villars [sic] home again is by open means and by the act of the Court of France, but I hope you agree too that any means, all means, must be tried rather than that this youth be abandoned to all the evil consequences of his mother's folly.[46]

Because the Tories were open to Whig charges of Jacobite leanings, they had to be especially careful not to risk scandals connected with Catholicism. Thus we find Bolingbroke writing to Prior again two weeks later, and bringing pressure to bear on Torcy:

Indeed we have reason to be provoked at this proceeding of the Papists. There have been lately attempts to decoy another young man of quality from Westminster School, and you may tell our friend [Torcy] that I shall proceed with so much heat against some of their people in a short time that he will be apt to take me for a Whig.[47]

Pressures of this sort proved effective, and in another two weeks we find Bolingbroke writing to Torcy to thank him for his efforts:

The news you have taken the pains to tell me, sir, by your letter of 25 of last month has given me a pleasure beyond description, nor can I better express my acknowledgments for it. In restoring to us the little run-away, whom his mother by an

45 British MSS. 49970.
46 Ibid.
47 Ibid.

excess of tenderness was going to ruin beyond redemption, you do an action worthy of yourself. Was there any feeling in the dead, and could those gentlemen communicate to us what they think, you would without doubt receive the late Earl of Jersey's compliments. As that cannot be, pray accept mine, as a friend and relation of the House of Villars.

Madame Jersey may rely on it . . . that I shall neglect nothing, as far as is in my power, for the education of her son, and his advancement. He whom I have chosen to receive him is a young man who serves me in quality of gentleman, and honest man for whom I can answer in everything. I hope Madame Jersey will put her son immediately into his hands, for I have ordered him to make haste back.[48]

Henry Villiers returned to England, eventually received his M.A. at Trinity College, Cambridge, and was ordained a priest in the Church of England. His parish was the quiet rural one of Frome Selwood in Somersetshire, where he lived quietly, dying without children in 1743.[49]

Meanwhile, in the great world of public events, time was overtaking Bolingbroke. Early in 1714 it became clear that James would not change his religion for the sake of becoming King of England. Bolingbroke's entreaties, the arguments of his adviser the Abbe Gaultier, who tried to persuade him that Rome would gain in the long run by his real or pretended apostasy—all left him unmoved. Bolingbroke played the only card that was left to him. Since James would not be obtained on Tory terms and since the Elector was irretrievably a Whig, the only course open was to get the entire machinery of government into Tory hands, and then bargain with the rival claimants to the throne. Even if George did succeed to the throne, Bolingbroke no doubt reasoned, he might hesitate to test the power even of a King against such an entrenched 'Tory system'. The success of such a policy required the removal of Harley, who trimmed and vacillated, and hoped to save some of his credit with the Whigs. Bolingbroke moved with energy and despatch: Steele was expelled from Commons for 'scandalous and seditious libels'; the Duke of Argyll was dismissed from all his offices; and the Schism Act was passed, which provided

[48] Ibid.
[49] See Venn's *Alumni Cantabrigiensis* (1927).

that the children of Dissenters be educated by schoolmasters licensed by the bishops. In foreign policy Bolingbroke negotiated a new treaty with France against the Whigs' ally Austria, 'a bold, original stroke of diplomacy, carried through with magnificent confidence and dexterity'.[50] As he wrote to the Lord Primate of Ireland on 24 July 1714: 'I know but one way of retrieving these disadvantages, and of preventing those misfortunes which every reasonable man sees before him, and which every honest man dreads; and it is to take hold of the present disposition which there seems to be to act a clear game as Tories, and on that foundation to establish the Queen's government.'[51]

Unfortunately for the success of this plan, time was running out. On 27 July, Bolingbroke at last prevailed on the Queen to dismiss her impenetrable Lord Treasurer, but she still withheld the White Staff from Bolingbroke—perhaps because, as Coxe says, she was offended by his profligacy and irreligion, or perhaps because illness had augmented her habitual indecisiveness. As the Earl of Mar wrote to his brother, the 'Lord T(reasurer) is now out, but I cannot tell you who is in, which is odd enough . . .'[52] In the midst of all this confusion alarming news arrived from Kensington. The Queen had been stricken by apoplexy, and a Council was summoned to the Palace. Bolingbroke was filled with apprehension, for he knew that Marlborough was on his way to England and that in a few hours the army would be under his orders, and he knew also that Stanhope and other Whigs had made preparations for seizing such strongpoints in the city as the Tower. At the Council meeting Bolingbroke proposed that Shrewsbury, a moderate, be given the White Staff, and Anne, as the last act of her life, handed it to him. It may be that Bolingbroke hoped to bring Shrewsbury over to his side after the Queen's death. If so, he was disappointed.

In the end all of Bolingbroke's schemes came to nothing. The Whigs, naturally, were united behind George, but Tory division over the succession was incurable. Many of the Tories favoured James whether or not he remained a Roman Catholic, but many others, more concerned for Protestantism than for

---

[50] Petrie, *Bolingbroke*, pp. 204–5; Plumb, *Sir Robert Walpole*, I, p. 195.
[51] British Museum MSS. 49970.
[52] H. M. C. Mar and Kellie MSS., p. 504, quoted in Petrie, *Bolingbroke*, p. 248.

Toryism, refused to support the accession of a Catholic King. Thus when Anne died Bolingbroke had not had time to establish an entrenched 'Tory system', and no other policy was available which could unite his followers. As he wrote to the Earl of Strafford on 13 August, 'the Queen's death was a very great surprise, for though I did not imagine she could hold out long, yet I hoped she would have got over the summer'.[53] In the event there was nothing for him to do but await the accession of George, and perhaps to hope that his leadership of the landed interest and those who were most zealous for the Church would count for something in the eyes of the new King. A message from the Elector himself to the Council of Regents put an end to uncertainty. Bolingbroke was to be summarily dismissed from his post as Secretary of State; his office was to be put under guard; his papers were to be sealed and confiscated. Bolingbroke was, he said, shocked by this treatment for two minutes, but, he added, 'the grief of my soul is this—I see plainly that the Tory party is gone'.[54]

At 6 p.m. on 8 September 1714 George I landed at Greenwich, to be received in the September twilight by the Whig grandees. Harley lingered on the fringes of the delegation, hoping for signs of favour. Bolingbroke did not bother to attend. 'I went', he wrote, 'about a month after the Queen's death, as soon as the seals were taken from me, into the country; and whilst I continued there, I felt the general disposition to Jacobitism increase daily among people of all ranks . . .'[55] It is difficult to estimate the real strength of Jacobitism at this time, and historians differ on the question, but Bolingbroke's impression that sympathy for James was increasing does not seem to have been an illusion, for a few months later spontaneous Jacobite disturbances reached proportions the Government considered ominous.[56] It was also clear to Bolingbroke, however, that he was in considerable personal danger. He knew that he would be the target of Whig resentment over the peace, and he could not tell how much they might find out about his negotiations with James. Though most of his private papers

[53] British Museum MSS. 49970.
[54] Letter to Atterbury, quoted in Plumb, *Sir Robert Walpole*, I, p. 198. Plumb, *Sir Robert Walpole*, I, p. 214.
[55] *Bolingbroke*, I, p. 128.
[56] J. H. Plumb, *Sir Robert Walpole*, I, p. 214.

were safely out of reach of the Government, there was one man who had shared his secrets whom the Whigs now had in their hands. Matthew Prior had recently arrived from France, and the representatives of Walpole and Stanhope had lost no time in attempting to curry his favour. Rumour had it that Prior planned to serve the Government as a witness against him. According to Coxe, Bolingbroke suspected that even Harley was co-operating against him and had heard that 'a resolution was taken to bring him to the scaffold'.[57] Marlborough is supposed to have warned him of the danger he was in; under the circumstances, his apprehension that his head might roll on the hill above the Tower of London cannot be dismissed as unfounded or cowardly.

On 26 March word spread in London that Bolingbroke had fled. At first no one believed it. He had been seen the previous evening in his box at Drury Lane, he had complimented the actors, he had taken seats for the next night's performance. But soon the truth was known. Between the acts he had slipped away to Dover, where a boat was waiting, and, disguised in a black wig and ordinary clothes, he was on his way to France.

[57] William Coxe, *Memoirs of the Life and Administration of Sir Robert Walpole, Earl of Oxford*, I (London, 1798), p. 128.

III

INSURRECTION AND EXILE

BOLINGBROKE's decision to serve James as Secretary of State, and to help organise the combined invasion and insurrection which might bring him to the throne, has been one focus of the controversy that always attends interpretation of his career. Until recently most historians have attacked him for this decision, arguing that he showed poor judgment in that James's cause was hopeless, and also that in serving James he revealed himself to be an unprincipled and even traitorous adventurer. Yet both of these charges are quite false. In the first place, as Plumb and other recent scholars have shown, the Jacobite cause was far from an unpromising one in the spring of 1715.[1] On the Continent the only powers in any way attached to George were Holland and Prussia. The sympathies of Spain were entirely on the side of James. French policy was complex, and aimed rather at fostering unrest in England than at a successful Jacobite restoration, but aid of various kinds from Louis XIV must have seemed a reasonable expectation; and Portuguese policy generally followed the lead of France.[2] By the Emperor, the accession of George was regarded with suspicion and jealousy.[3] In Scotland discontent was general, and Ireland would have greeted Jacobite success with unmixed joy. Unrest smouldered in the English countryside, and agents of James were busy organising it into a national movement against the Hanoverians. Riots of a Jacobite coloration had taken place in London. Mobs in Lancashire had cried 'Down

---

[1] J. H. Plumb, *Sir Robert Walpole*, I (Boston, 1956), pp. 213–14.
[2] Sir Charles Petrie, *The Jacobite Movement* (London, 1959), p. 88.
[3] J. Churton Collins, *Bolingbroke: a Historical Study* (London, 1886), p. 117.

with the Rump', and there were grave disturbances in Shropshire, Colchester, and elsewhere.[4] As Petrie concludes, the tide of Hanoverian unpopularity was rising, 'and an insurrection in the West, combined with that of Forster in Lancashire, of Kenmure in the Lowlands, and of Mar in the Highlands, might well have brought the Stuarts back to the throne'.[5]

Nor can Bolingbroke really be charged with disloyalty or lack of principle in his decision to serve James. Although George was now, by Act of Parliament, King of England, many of his subjects regarded the dynastic claims of James as having greater validity, and still more would have agreed with Chesterton that George 'was simply something stuffed into a hole in the wall by English aristocrats, who practically admitted that they were simply stuffing it with rubbish'.[6] Even such leading Whigs as Marlborough, Shrewsbury, and Walpole had taken care to cultivate James's favour through secret correspondence. Bolingbroke's own explanation of his motives, moreover, is perfectly consistent with his conduct, and is supported by the most recent research into the matter.[7] Throughout his career Bolingbroke's political position had been based on the principle that the power of the financial oligarchy posed a threat to the other interests in the community. He considered the Whigs to be the instruments of the oligarchy, and when it became clear that George's bias in favour of the Whig groups could not be overcome he took the only course available to him. As he says in the *Letter to Wyndham*, he conceived of himself in 1715 as acting not as a Jacobite, but as the servant of the Tory party. It is difficult, therefore, to accept Petrie's explanation of Bolingbroke's flight from England—that he temporarily lost his head —or the imputation of other historians that his joining James was an act of desperate folly. He may well have felt that he was playing his last card, but it was a good one. The failure of the

[4] J. H. Plumb, *Sir Robert Walpole*, I, p. 214.

[5] Sir Charles Petrie, *Bolingbroke* (London, 1937), p. 269.

[6] G. K. Chesterton, *A Short History of England* (New York, 1917), p. 219.

[7] See particularly the following articles by H. N. Fieldhouse: 'Bolingbroke's Share in the Jacobite Intrigue of 1710–1714', *English Historical Review*, LII (1937), pp. 637–62, and 'Bolingbroke and the d'Iberville Correspondence, August 1714– June 1715', *English Historical Review*, LII (1937), pp. 637–82. Fieldhouse shows that prior to 1713 Bolingbroke was not involved to any exceptional degree with Jacobitism, and that his subsequent Jacobite association was, as he claimed, intended to serve the Tory interest.

'15, total though it was, may not have been due to any faults in the conception of the scheme or to inadequate means, but rather to the fact that the widely scattered Jacobite forces and highly individualistic leaders failed during the crucial weeks to co-ordinate their efforts. Thus Ormonde's precipitate journey to France, and Mar's premature raising of James's standard, were instrumental in bringing about the Jacobite defeat.[8]

One of James's first acts upon returning to France from Scotland was to dismiss Bolingbroke from office, and around this, as around so many of the events of Bolingbroke's career, clouds of unresolved controversy have whirled. James might be supposed to have needed a scapegoat for the defeat, and to find one is a normal recourse in politics; it is a way of saving the cause itself. Yet Bolingbroke's dismissal has a sudden and improvised character, more the flavour of the personal than of the Machiavellian. One story has it that Bolingbroke dined with James, who assured him of his goodwill, and retired, later on, at about one in the morning. At nine the next day Ormonde arrived, demanding from him the Seals of office. Had Bolingbroke, as Coxe thinks, made fun of James while drunk, causing James to send Ormonde to him the next morning?[9] In support of this is the report that the Queen Mother, Mary of Modena, begged Bolingbroke to remain with the Jacobites, saying that matters might be reconciled.[10] The official explanation of the dismissal is contained in a memorandum James wrote in 1716 charging Bolingbroke with culpable failures in procuring arms and other supplies:

> The removal of the Earl of Bolingbroke may perhaps appear unaccountable and unexpected to our friends in England, but it has long been forseen, at least thought necessary, by all who interest themselves in France for the King's Restauration . . . It was near five months from the fifteenth of September, on which the Duke of Mar set up the King's standard, till the fourth of February, on which the King and he were forced to embark at Montrose for France. Yet in all this time not one musket or pound of powder (except 1400 weight sent from

---

[8] See Petrie, *Bolingbroke*, Ch. VIII.

[9] William Coxe, *Memoirs of the Life and Administration of Sir Robert Walpole, Earl of Orford*, I (London, 1798), p. 200.

[10] Ibid.

Harvre the later end of January round Ireland and not yet arrived) notwithstanding the most pressing instances and earnest solicitations of the Duke of Mar, and that above a dozen ships sent by Lord Bolingbroke from France arrived in Scotland within that period . . . The Chief of this present Court have all along had a very bad opinion both of the discretion and integrity of Lord Bolingbroke . . .[11]

Yet Bolingbroke, whatever his personal failings, had always been a superb administrator, and we have, moreover, the testimony of the Duke of Berwick, James's half-brother and one of the most able military men of his time, that Bolingbroke had done all within his power:

One must have lost one's reason if one did not see the enormous blunder made by King James in dismissing the only Englishman he had able to manage his affairs, for whatever may be said by some persons of more passion than judgment, it is admitted by all in England that there have been few greater ministers than Bolingbroke. I was in part a witness how Bolingbroke acted for King James whilst he managed his affairs, and I owe him the justice to say, that he left nothing undone of what he could do; he moved heaven and earth to obtain supplies, but was always put off by the Court of France; and tho he saw through their pretexts and complained of them, yet there was no other power to which he could apply.[12]

Another hypothesis involves Bolingbroke's relations with Claudine de Tencin, an ex-nun, probably introduced to him by Matthew Prior, who had become his mistress while he was negotiating the Treaty of Utrecht.[13] When he returned to Paris as an exile in 1715 he renewed the relationship with her, despite the fact that she had meanwhile become the mistress of the Abbé Dubois, later a cardinal, who for financial reasons was a strong supporter of the Hanoverian at St. James's. At the very least, Bolingbroke was highly indiscreet in sharing a mistress with this French Minister; and, notoriously reckless in his confidences with women, he may have told Claudine things that later found their way via Dubois to London. The Government, in any case,

[11] British Museum MSS. 38851.
[12] Ibid.
[13] Petrie, *The Jacobite Movement*, pp. 280-3.

was seldom in the dark about Jacobite plans. Yet theories of this sort seem less important, on balance, than the obvious difference in temper between Bolingbroke and St. Germains. Urbane, sceptical, dissolute, Bolingbroke had offended Anne, and her dislike for him very likely had kept Harley in office until it was too late; how much more must his personality have irritated James, who before his departure from Rome in 1717 'climbed the holy stairs upon his knees in presence of a multitude of people, who were much pleased with his devotion, [and] was presented by Signior Bianchi with a Golden Cross adorned with medals, and a piece of wood of the pretended true Cross . . .'[14] This was not Bolingbroke's mode. Writing to Horatio Walpole, Lord Stair, English Ambassador at Paris, cited Bolingbroke's attitude as the real reason for the break:

> . . . poor Harry is turned out from being Secretary of State, and the seals are given to Mar, and they use poor Harry most unmercifully, and call him knave and traitor, and God knows what. I believe all poor Harry's fault was, that he could not play his part with a grave enough face. He could not help laughing now and then at such Kings and Queens . . . I would not have you laugh, Mr. Walpole, for all this is very serious.[15]

Despite James's memorandum, then, Bolingbroke's dismissal has an impulsive look about it. Berwick was on his side, and the Queen Mother asked him to remain; perhaps some incautious remarks, reflecting his actual attitudes, had deeply offended James; in any case, he replied to the Queen Mother that he was a free man, and that he wished his arm might rot off if he ever drew his sword or employed his pen in their service again,[16] and immediately, through his friend Sir William Wyndham, began to urge the Tories at home to avoid entanglement with James. 'Nothing', he wrote to Wyndham on September 13, 1716,

> can be so desperate as the circumstances of affairs, nothing so miserable as the characters, nothing so weak as the measures . . . Let me . . . conjure you on no account whatever to

---

[14] British Museum MSS. 38851: Holograph letter from James Wilson to Lord Marischal, 29 August 1717.
[15] British Museum MSS. 38851.
[16] Coxe, I, 200.

enter into any measure, till by some means or other we have contrived to meet . . . Keep yourself till then absolutely independent of all engagements.[17]

This letter hints at a new move by the Jacobites, who are 'very sanguine'. Bolingbroke forwarded it to London *unsealed*, knowing that it would be read. Craggs, the Postmaster-General, brought it to Townshend, who showed it to the King. It seems clear that at this point Bolingbroke had two things in mind. He had dismissed the idea of a Jacobite restoration and was trying to keep the domestic Tories clear of entanglements that would handicap them, and he had begun to manoeuvre for his own return to England. If the oligarchy were to be fought, it would have to be done at home.

After the death of his first wife in 1718 Bolingbroke bought a small estate near Orleans called La Source, so named for the Loiret, which rose in its grounds. There he brought the Marquise de Villette, whom he eventually married. The widow of the Marquis de Villette and the niece of Madame de Maintenon, Marie-Claire Deschamps de Marcilly, though upwards of 40, had lost none of the grace and vivacity that had made her the delight of the polished circle at Versailles in which she moved. In her Bolingbroke found the first woman he had ever really loved, and he remained devoted to her until her death in 1750, the year before his own. And so, despite his exile, life at La Source had its compensations. He described his grounds as 'the most beautiful place that Nature ever adorned', and wrote to Swift that he had in his wood the 'biggest and clearest spring perhaps in Europe, which forms before it leaves the park a more beautiful river than any which flows in Greek or Latin verse'.[18] Here at La Source, free from political involvement, he was able to devote himself to the studies which many years before had given him so much pleasure. Though he loved power and the life of action, there was a reflective side of his character, a deep attachment to the pleasures of thought and the beauties of language. As he wrote of himself in *On the Use of Retirement and Study*:

[17] British Museum MSS. 2291.
[18] *The Correspondence of Jonathan Swift*, ed. F. Elrington Ball, III (London, 1910–14), p. 93.

There has been something always ready to whisper in my ear, whilst I run the course of pleasure and business, '*Solve senescentum mature sanus equum.*' But my genius, unlike the genius of Socrates, whispered so softly, that very often I heard him not, in the hurry of those passions by which I was transported. Some calmer hours there were: in them I hearkened to him. Reflection had often its turn, and the love of study and the desire of knowledge have never quite abandoned me, I am not therefore entirely unprepared for the life I will lead, and it is not without reason that I promise myself more satisfaction in the latter part of it, than I ever knew in the former.[19]

Voltaire visited him at La Source, as did Madame du Deffand and the young Abbé Alari, who was to become Sous-Precepteur to Louis XIV. Voltaire found Bolingbroke to be an extraordinary person: 'I have found in this eminent Englishman', he wrote to his friend Thiriot, 'all the learning of his country and all the politeness of ours. I never heard our language spoken with more energy and justice. This man, who has been all his life immersed in pleasure and business, has, however, found time for learning everything and retaining everything. He is well acquainted with the history of the ancient Egyptians as well as with that of England. He loves the poetry of England, France, Italy . . .'[20] When he visited Paris, Bolingbroke found time to frequent the discussions of the Société d'Entresol, a literary and philosophical club founded by Alari and attended by many of the current illuminati, among whom M. de Pouilly, the philosopher, and Brook Taylor, the brilliant English scientist and mathematician, provided welcome guidance for Bolingbroke's studies. During this period, as Churton Collins observes, Bolingbroke 'became identified with almost every movement of the public mind in Europe, with political opinion, with polite letters, with the speculations of science, with the progress of free thought, with historical and metaphysical discussion'.[21]

While Bolingbroke thus passed quietly and pleasantly his years of exile abroad, events in England were preparing the way to political power for his old rival Walpole, and transforming

---

[19] *The Works of Lord Bolingbroke*, II (Philadelphia, 1841), p. 345.
[20] *Voltaire's Correspondence*, ed. Theodore Besterman, I (Geneva, 1953), p. 178.
[21] Petrie, *Bolingbroke*, p. 93.

the terms of political controversy. Accordingly, when Bolingbroke finally did secure his pardon in 1723 he returned to a
political scene quite different from the one that had existed
under Anne. Before 1714, broadly speaking, the parties had
represented rival principles—the Tories associated with Church,
King, and the landed interest, as opposed to the Whiggish
leaning to toleration, contract theories of government, and
commerce. Under the first two Georges, as the likelihood of a
Stuart restoration faded, the dynastic question ceased to be
the focus of controversy, and the terms 'Tory' and 'Whig' came
to mean a good deal less. As one historian puts it, the 'parties
dissolved into the confusion of "connexions" linked by patronage and kinship, and "interests" influenced by common
economic concerns'.[22] Yet out of this confusion the older issues
emerged in different terms. No longer able to hope for a Stuart
monarch, opponents of the oligarchy shifted their attention to a
Parliamentary struggle, and their position expressed itself in a
campaign for the 'independence' of Parliament from the influence of a Whiggish Court. Previously, the Crown had represented the 'national interest'; under the first two Georges it
seemed to analysts like Bolingbroke that the national interest
would be represented by Parliament or not at all. To understand this transformation, and to appreciate the reasons under-
lying the bitterness of the Opposition campaign against Walpole
and the oligarchy, it will be necessary to examine very briefly
the circumstances under which that remarkable politician rose
to supreme power.

Walpole's emergence was made possible by the failure of the
South Sea Company in the summer of 1720, and at the time
to a large extent was unforeseeable.[23] In the years following
the death of Anne in 1714 the Sunderland-Stanhope faction of the
Whigs had entrenched itself in power. Indeed, in May 1720 the
King, fearing the power of the ministry, actually considered
establishing in its place a weak coalition of Tories and such
disaffected Whigs as Walpole and Townshend, but Sunderland,
sensing his danger, diverted Walpole with the lucrative but

[22] G. E. Mingay, *English Landed Society in the Eighteenth Century* (London, 1963),
p. 115.
[23] The following account of Walpole's emergence follows C. R. Realey, *The
Early Opposition to Sir Robert Walpole* (Kansas, 1932), and J. H. Plumb, *Sir Robert
Walpole*, I (Boston, 1956).

politically insignificant post of Paymaster of the Forces. With Walpole thus neutralised, Parliament rose on 11 June 1720, and did not meet again until 8 December. During the summer events changed these power relations drastically. Walpole had repaired for the warm months to his Norfolk estate, Houghton. Meanwhile the London financial world was caught in a spiral of wild inflation, the centre of which was the South Sea Company, a finance company which had been authorised by the Government to take over part of the national debt and liquidate it by selling stocks. Backed by the credit of the Government, South Sea stocks rose spectacularly in price. 'The topic of conversation when members of the substantial classes met', writes W. T. Laprade, 'was how much each had made. From the Prince of Wales to the humblest merchant whose name had prestige to persuade his friends, all were utilised by the promoters, who left few tricks untried in selling stocks . . . Rumours poured through coffee-houses and the press. Great ladies gave orders from tea tables adjacent to the exchange.'[24] Tables had to be placed in the street to accommodate those crowding to trade in stocks. The 'madness of stock-jobbing is inconceivable', wrote Edward Harley to his brother, and even the directors of the South Sea Company began to be alarmed at the success of the scheme. Many others, like Defoe, writing in Mist's *Journal*, foresaw disaster, and warned 'country gentlemen and rich farmers' said to be on the roads from all parts of the kingdom, each 'expecting no less than to ride down again in his coach and six', that although there would be some 'prizes' there would be 'many more blanks'.[25] Such warnings, however, went unheeded as South Sea stock rose to the point where a £100 share was selling for £1,000, and paper millionaires crowded the coffee-houses. As was inevitable, the price of the stock dropped sharply as soon public confidence ebbed, and in September 1720, as investors panicked, the entire financial structure of the country appeared threatened. On 19 September, Walpole, still a minor member of the ministry, returned to London to confer with the other Ministers on the crisis. Authorities differ on the importance of Walpole's role in this conference,

[24] William Thomas Laprade, *Public Opinion and Politics in Eighteenth Century England* (New York, 1936), p. 232.
[25] Ibid., 230.

but in any case he stayed in London only ten days before returning to Houghton. There has been much speculation about his motives for returning to Houghton, but whatever his reasons it was a shrewd move, for, as Plumb observes, its effect was to dissociate him from the crisis in the public mind. 'This may not have been a conscious motive in Walpole's decision,' writes Plumb, 'for politicians are often led to take steps which afterwards reek of Machiavellian foresight. Yet it is curious that no sooner had Walpole got back home than his name was on everyone's lips.'[26] It was recalled that he had opposed the South Sea Bill, though he had done so only for reasons of partisan politics, and it happened that he was comparatively untainted by complicity in the questionable practices of the Company. There is no evidence, however, that he had actually foreseen disaster. Nevertheless, he was widely looked to as the man who could lead the country out of the crisis.

When Parliament met again in December, Walpole made an important decision. He would oppose in every way at his disposal the popular demand that those responsible for the financial disaster be severely punished. Walpole was shrewd enough to realise that the relations between the South Sea Company, the ministry, and the Court would not bear close Parliamentary scrutiny. He knew, too, that in eighteenth-century politics Royal favour was an important source of political power, and that to support the public demand for the disgrace of the King's Ministers and mistresses would scarcely endear him to the King. Historians agree that Walpole's 'moderate' course in respect to the punishment of the guilty, though it flouted justice, was probably best for the country in the long run. Popular indignation, the unpopularity of the Hanoverians, and the desperation of the many ruined in the crash, could have resulted in revolution and a renewal of civil war. But though Walpole's policy of protecting the ministry and the Court may have been wise in the long run, it earned him the hatred of the majority of the people and the nickname of 'Robert Skreen'—the screen of the guilty. But he could afford to disregard their indignation. He now had the support of the Crown and of the great magnates, far more valuable assets than popularity in eighteenth-century politics.[27]

[26] J. H. Plumb, *Sir Robert Walpole*, I, p. 323.
[27] This estimate depends on Realey and Plumb.

In the country at large, however, Walpole's reputation touched bottom in January 1721. Demonstrations took place in the streets against 'the screen'. In the House the debate always seemed to go against Walpole's policy, but he inevitably got the votes he needed. Large sums of Court money saved the men the Court wanted saved. Fifty members who could not find it in their consciences to vote for the clearance of Charles Stanhope were persuaded to abstain: Stanhope was cleared by a majority of three. Knight, secretary of the South Sea Company, fled the country, probably taking with him, to the relief of the ministry, much incriminating evidence. 'The people of London were enraged; riots and disorders expressed their impotent frustration at what they rightly considered a travesty of justice.'[28] Prior wrote to Swift that 'conditions were wilder than St. Anthony's dream'. Even more outrageous than acquitting the guilty, in the eyes of many people, was Walpole's cold-blooded willingness to let minor figures be sacrificed. When Aislabie appeared 'submissive and pathetic before the Commons, Walpole's corner sat mute as fishes', and Aislabie went to the Tower.[29] Despite the fact that Walpole was able to manage Sunderland's acquittal, his position as leading Minister was damaged, and Walpole's strengthened, for an embarrassingly large number of dissenting votes was cast. When the crisis began Walpole had been a minor member of the Sunderland-Stanhope ministry; by the end of March the Walpole faction had achieved parity. By the end of April 1722 two things had happened which put Walpole in control.[30] First, Sunderland died suddenly. Widespread rumours that he had died of poison suggest the quality of Walpole's reputation at the time. Of equal importance was the general election of 1722, from which Walpole's opponents had hoped much, but which gave him more power than he had enjoyed in the old Parliament.

Now a good deal of corruption, or vote-buying, was normal in eighteenth-century elections, but the election of 1722 was not a normal one. Contemporaries seem to have felt that it brought something new into English politics, and that corruption new in kind and unprecedented in degree was employed.

[28] J. H. Plumb, *Sir Robert Walpole*, I, p. 342.
[29] Quoted by Realey, p. 26.
[30] J. H. Plumb, *Sir Robert Walpole*, I, p. 347.

When the Septennial Parliament was drawing to a close the Court interest decided that the power of those who had done its work, such as Walpole, would have to be strengthened. The expectations of the country were decidedly different. When the session ended 'bonfires, illuminations, and ringing of bells indicated the joy of the people in what was regarded as an "extraordinary deliverance", and everywhere went up the song celebrating the demise of the Septennial Parliament, "Down Amongst the Dead Men Let Them Lie" '.[31] On election day, in Westminster, the Court candidates had to be protected by the guards, so strong was the feeling against them. The hopes of Tories and other groups in opposition ran high; yet when the returns were in the position of the Court interest was stronger than ever, that of the Opposition virtually hopeless.

How this result was achieved is perfectly clear. In previous elections popular feelings had played an important role in determining the outcome. Though only a minority actually voted, it reflected to a considerable degree the mood of the country at large. Candidates for office might 'cultivate their borough'; still, as Petrie observes, if they bribed they bribed their own money, and Tories could spend as much as Whigs.[32] In the general election of 1722, however, 'methods used apparently for the first time by an English government' ensured that Court candidates would be returned whatever the state of public opinion.[33] The King 'flatters himself', wrote Destouches, the French Ambassador, 'that by means of much labour and money devoted to the country districts he will be able to make the elections turn out in favour of the Whigs'.[34] Solicitors disposing of unprecedented sums went about the country rounding up votes, and even went so far as to advertise for them in the public Press.[35] Dr. Stratford wrote of 'prodigious spending', and, what is even more significant as far as public feeling is concerned, he observed that a new class of people, disposing of funds evidently derived from financial speculation, were active in the elections.[36] Inevitably, the Duke of Newcastle was widely

[31] Realey, p. 107.
[32] Petrie, *Bolingbroke*, p. 128.
[33] Realey, p. 107.
[34] Realey, p. 108.
[35] Realey, p. 109.
[36] Realey, p. 111.

influential. He 'spent hugely on Sunderland's behalf both in Sussex and in Nottingham. He made long, slow electoral tours in which he was rarely sober for days on end, but the outcome was outstanding success for his candidates . . .'[37] Even Walpole's admirers were shocked by the methods employed to win this election. Young Sir Philip Yorke, using a phrase that would echo through *The Beggar's Opera* and *Jonathan Wild*, remarked that 'the great man' had not been 'sufficiently delicate about the decision of elections'.[38] This election ensured the stability of the Hanoverian dynasty, and cleared Walpole's way to supreme power, but the Government had won against the feelings of the nation, and it had used unprecedented methods to do so.

After the election of 1722 significant opposition to the ruling faction evaporated. A record of consistent failure against the Walpole monolith discouraged most potential opponents. The exposure of the Jacobite plot and the banishment of Atterbury disposed of others. Sporadic individual intrigues came to nothing. The brilliant Carteret, who could speak to the King in German, might manoeuvre to replace Walpole in the King's favour; he was ruined by the affair of Wood's halfpence in Ireland. Thus, ironically enough, Swift's campaign in the *Drapier's Letters*, by ruining Carteret, served in the end to strengthen Walpole, whom Swift detested. By luck, by 'management', the 'great man' succeeded in 'springing the mine' under potential rivals. At the end of 1725 Walpole found himself in complete control of every branch of the Government. Opposition leaders were dead, retired, or banished from politics. Places of influence were filled by Walpolians. As Realey says, 'the Church was under a growing control, the press was harmless, the government of London weakened, and the Jacobites broken'.[39] In summing up Walpole's career, Lecky states powerfully the case against him, observing that although previous politicians had resorted to corruption when crises arose, it was left to Walpole 'to organise corruption as a system, and make it the normal process of parliamentary government. It was his settled practice to maintain his parliamentary majority, not by attracting to his ministry, great orators, great writers, great financiers, or great statesmen,

[37] J. H. Plumb, *Sir Robert Walpole*, I, 377–8.
[38] Realey, p. 115.
[39] Realey, p. 153.

not by effecting any combination or coalition of parties, by identifying himself with any great object of popular desire, or by winning to his side young men in whose character or ability he could trace the promise of future eminence, but simply by engrossing borough influence and extending the patronage of the Crown. Material motives were the only ones he recognised.'[40] Even sympathetic historians have noted that Walpole's aversion to excellence was almost pathological, and that he systematically alienated every talented man who attempted to ally himself with the Government. One is forced to conclude, therefore, that the charges of his opponents that he was undermining the Constitution by destroying the independence of Parliament, and that his methods were bringing the national Government itself into contempt, had a solid basis in fact. The most recent historians, on the other hand, have been kinder to Walpole. Looking back on his régime, they have been able to evaluate him in the light of later events, such as the development of the party system and the growing importance of the House of Commons. It can even be argued that in his handling of the crisis after the collapse of the South Sea Company he 'showed qualities of statesmanship of the highest order', and preserved the structure of Government 'at a time when it could easily have dissolved in chaos'.[41] There is much to be said for this side of the story, but it should not cause us to gloss over the truths Walpole's contemporaries saw at close hand. The election of 1722, for example, which did much to create the image of a corrupt Walpole, is treated perfunctorily by Plumb and Morley. Modern historians may take comfort from the fact that the dire results predicted by Walpole's contemporary critics did not occur; but it may be that they were forestalled by the articulate and eventually powerful Opposition formed by Bolingbroke and his political and literary allies.

In May 1723, after eight years of exile, Bolingbroke was at last able to secure his pardon. A large bribe to the Duchess of Kendall helped pave the way, but the political rationale for the pardon undoubtedly was Bolingbroke's usefulness in persuading the Tories to break with Jacobitism, a service he per-

---

[40] W. E. H. Lecky, *England in the Eighteenth Century*, I (New York, 1890), pp. 399–400.
[41] J. H. Plumb, *Sir Robert Walpole*, I, p. 380.

formed in his *Letter to Sir William Wyndham*. The attainder was removed from Bolingbroke, and his estates restored, but Walpole managed to have withheld from him the right to sit in Parliament. Bolingbroke's political activities in the years that followed had therefore to be confined to the role of intellectual leader and strategist of the Opposition. He settled at Dawley, an estate near Pope's house at Twickenham, and there attracted to him a circle of poets, pamphleteers, and ambitious young politicians, united by their dedication to the destruction of Walpole's political machine.

IV

THEORIST OF THE OPPOSITION

I F THE great achievement of the early part of Bolingbroke's career was the Peace of Utrecht, that of the later years was the role he played in shaping the Opposition to Walpole. Under the most unpromising political circumstances, and prohibited from taking his seat in the House of Lords, he was able to organise the divergent Opposition groups into an effective Parliamentary force, and, beyond that, he developed a theory of Parliamentary Opposition, and set forth constitutional principles, that were to have a permanent influence on English politics.

The political leaders available to Bolingbroke for his campaign against Walpole were as diverse a lot as can be imagined. William Pulteney, an able economist and a brilliant orator, was a lifelong Whig and had no important principled differences with Walpole. Fiercely ambitious, he broke with the ministry in 1725 when Walpole passed him over for Secretary of State in favour of the dull but more subservient Newcastle. Pulteney had taken account of Walpole's aversion to men of talent, and drawn the logical conclusion that the only way for him to advance himself was to bring about the fall of the leading Minister. The Earl of Chesterfield, also a firm Whig, but an accomplished intriguer, likewise hoped for better things from Walpole's fall. In addition, there was a small band of Hanoverian Tories led by Sir William Wyndham, long a friend and disciple of Bolingbroke, but these were uneasy about alliance with Opposition Whigs, and, as 'country gentlemen', felt superior to them. William Shippen, Pope's 'honest Shippen', bluff and forthright, led the thirty-odd Parliamentary Jacobites who hoped to restore

the Stuarts by legal methods, but these were cool to Bolingbroke, who had been dismissed by James amid acrimonious
charges and counter-charges. Such groups had little in common
besides an antipathy to Walpole and his Government, and this
circumstance limited the rhetorical possibilities available to
Bolingbroke in his political propaganda as well as the kinds of
issues on which a fight might be made in Parliament. Accordingly, he conceived of his campaign in terms of attack—on
Walpole personally, on 'corruption', and on Government by a
'faction'. Yet, despite the difficulties imposed upon him by the
heterogeneous forces he had to work with, he devoted to the
campaign, in Disraeli's phrase, 'all the energies of his Protean
mind', striving at every opportunity to realise his own demanding ideal of Opposition. 'They who affect to head an Opposition,' he wrote, 'or to make any considerable figure in it, must
be equal, at least, to those whom they oppose; I do not say, in
parts only, but in application and industry, and the fruits of
both, information, knowledge, and a certain constant prepared-
ness for all the events that may arise. Every administration is a
system of conduct: Opposition, therefore, should be a system
of conduct likewise; an opposite, but not a dependent system.'
Though Bolingbroke, Pulteney, and their followers achieved
only an imperfect version of this ideal, we may easily recognise
in it the lineaments of the Opposition as conceived by Burke
and Rockingham, and, beyond that, by modern Parliamen-
tarians.

Bolingbroke's management of the campaign against Walpole
recalled the strategy he and Harley had employed in 1709–10,
combining Court intrigue with a ferocious propaganda attack
in the public Press. In the autumn of 1726—as we will see, a
momentous year—a new Opposition newspaper was launched.
Taking over the fading *Country-Gentleman*, renamed *The Craftsman*, and installing Nicholas Amhurst as editor, the leaders of
the Opposition, with Bolingbroke doing much of the actual
writing, brought to bear on Walpole the most devastating
invective to appear since *The Examiner*.[1] 'Week after week
Walpole and his ministry were subjected to an endless stream
of vilification and criticism which made not only England but

---

[1] J. H. Plumb, *Sir Robert Walpole*, II (London, 1960), p. 141.

Europe roar with delight.'[2] But while Bolingbroke reproduced the strategy of *The Examiner* with *The Craftsman*, and while intrigues with the King's mistress Henrietta Howard replaced those of fifteen years before with Abigail Masham, Bolingbroke gathered about him, as he had in the days of the Scriblerus Club, a glittering literary coterie.

Alexander Pope was a frequent visitor at Dawley, where, to his amusement, he found Bolingbroke posing as a gentleman farmer. 'I now hold the pen for my Lord Bolingbroke,' he wrote to Swift in June 1728,

> who is reading your letter between two Haycocks, but his attention is sometimes diverted by casting his eyes on the clouds, not in admiration of what you say, but for fear of a shower . . . As to the return of his health and vigour, were you here, you might enquire of his Hay-makers; but as to his temperance, I can answer that (for one whole day) we have had nothing for dinner but mutten-broth, beans and bacon, and a Barn-door fowl.
>
> Now his Lordship is run after his Cart, I have a moment left to myself to tell you that I overheard him yesterday agree with a painter for £200 to paint his country-hall with Trophies of Rakes, spades, prongs, etc., and other ornaments merely to countenance his calling this place a farm.[3]

Bolingbroke was most at home in London and in the capitals of Europe, and no doubt his appearing to be a gentleman farmer had in it an element of affectation. But he also was genuinely drawn to rural life; in France he had chosen not to live in Paris; and so Pope's ironies may be at least partially misplaced. In any case, Bolingbroke had a profound influence on Pope, the greatest poet of the century. Pope did not, as has been supposed, take over Bolingbroke's philosophy for *An Essay on Man*, yet there can be no doubt that it was Bolingbroke who turned the poet to philosophical subjects.[4] It was Bolingbroke who in their 'philosophical conversations' encouraged the poet to stoop to truth and moralise his song; and one cannot doubt that it was Bolingbroke's influence that helped to make the

---

[2] Ibid.

[3] *The Correspondence of Alexander Pope*, ed. George Sherburn, II (Oxford, 1956), p. 503.

[4] *An Essay on Man*, ed. Maynard Mack (New Haven, 1951), pp. xxvi–xxxi.

Horatian imitations so political, and the estimate of England at mid-century, as expressed in the fourth book of the *Dunciad*, so profoundly pessimistic.

The campaign against Walpole had other literary aspects. Indeed, a law seemed to be operating, in which the defeated party scored the imaginative triumphs. As we have seen, *The Craftsman* began to appear on the London streets in 1726; the same year Swift returned to England, bringing with him the manuscript of *Gulliver's Travels*, and the Tory supporters of Anne had a reunion at Pope's estate at Twickenham. Gay was working on his *Fables* and *The Beggar's Opera*, and Pope on the first three books of *The Dunciad*. All would appear within two years, and all participated in the spirit of the opposition to Walpole. It required no great skill at deciphering allegory, for example, to apply the tale told in Gay's seventh Fable to current political affairs. In the animal kingdom, the Lion, 'tired with state affairs', names the Fox his regent. Another fox steps forth and delivers a panegyric on this new power in the State: 'What blessings must attend the nation/ Under this good administration.' A Goose, however, standing apart from the crowd, interprets these events for us:

> When'er I hear a knave commend,
> He bids me shun his worthy friend.
> What praise! What mighty commendation!
> But twas a fox who spoke the oration.
> Foxes this government may prize,
> As gentle, plentiful, and wise;
> If they enjoy the sweets, 'tis plain
> We geese must feel a tyrant reign.[5]

The suggestion that Walpole's Government was the rule of a Machiavellian tyrant (a Lion and a Fox) would not have been lost on readers of the *Fables*, and the Machiavellian reference for Walpole, deepened and complicated, was later to be central to *The Idea of a Patriot King*. The other works, too, embodied an attack on England as it had emerged under Walpole and the Hanoverians. *The Beggar's Opera* ridicules a society in which money is the highest good, and *Gulliver's Travels* depicts an England in precipitous decline, the victim of a politics of faction,

[5] *The Poetical Works of John Gay*, ed. G. C. Faber (London, 1926), p. 215.

populated by money-grubbers and bemused by frivolous scientism.

Certainly Bolingbroke, like the other leading figures in the Opposition, was motivated by the desire for personal power. Even Pope and Swift, who could bring to bear on the leading Minister the most devastating ridicule, would also flatter him personally and solicit favours.[6] Yet beyond the intrigue and the double-dealing the Opposition was making a powerful case against the Government. As Plumb has pointed out, England had begun to drift into oligarchical rule following the Glorious Revolution, and gradually resistance to the oligarchy had faded. 'For a time in the reigns of William and Anne, the attempt to stop the glissade into corruption was a vital concern of many members . . . Harley's solicitude for the purity of elections needs little explanation; the country gentlemen who supported [measures against corruption] numbered nearly two hundred. The spread of corruption and the growth of oligarchy steadily diminished this number until it reached about one hundred, a figure at which it remained for the rest of the eighteenth century.'[7] It was this drift into oligarchical rule that Bolingbroke resisted. In his view the balance of the Constitution depended upon the independence of its three parts:

A King of Great Britain is that supreme magistrate who has a negative voice in the legislature. He is entrusted with the executive power, and several other powers and privileges, which we call prerogatives, are annxed to this trust. The two Houses of Parliament have their rights and privileges, some of which are common to both, others particular to each . . . If the legislative as well as the executive power was wholly in the King, as in some countries, he would be absolute . . . It is this division of power, these distinct privileges attributed to the King, the Lords, and the Commons, which constitute a limited monarchy . . . If any one of the three . . . should at any time usurp more power than the law gives, or make an ill use of a legal power, the other two parts may, by uniting their strength, reduce this power into its proper bonds . . . This is that balance which has been so much talked of . . . This proposition is therefore true: that in a constitution like

[6] J. H. Plumb, *Sir Robert Walpole*, II, p. 175.
[7] J. H. Plumb, *Sir Robert Walpole*, I, p. 65.

ours, the safety of the whole depends on the balance of the parts.[8]

For Bolingbroke to espouse this theory may at first seem suspicious. Under Anne he had been more royalist than the monarch: 'What passed on Thursday in the House of Commons', he had written to Strafford, 'will I hope, show people abroad, as well as at home, that no merit, no grandeur, no riches, can excuse or save any, who sets himself up in opposition to the Queen.'[9] But the political aspect of Parliament and Crown had altered after 1715. Under Anne, resistance to the oligarchy had possessed at least the sympathy of the Crown, but under the Hanoverians, as Bolingbroke saw it, the Crown itself was the creature of the oligarchy: only an independent Parliament, informed by an aroused public opinion, could represent the interests of the whole of England. Bolingbroke saw the power of money as even more menacing than the abuse of the Royal prerogative formerly had been; looking back on the campaign against Walpole, he wrote to Wyndham in 1736 that they had tried to serve "our country, and ourselves, by demolishing that power that is become tyranny in the paws of the greatest bear, and the greatest jackanapes upon earth . . . The corruption now employed is at least as dangerous as the prerogative formerly employed. Against prerogative, the public alarm, and the opposition of parliaments, were a real security. Against corruption, extended as it is, what security is there?"[10] As he had done under Anne, Bolingbroke was struggling to prevent the domination of England by an oligarchy he viewed as emerging as a result of the Glorious Revolution. 'If you hinder the consequences of the revolution', he wrote to Wyndham in 1736, 'from destroying that constitution which the revolution was meant to improve and perpetuate, I shall end my days in the obscurity of retreat with far greater satisfaction than the splendour of the world ever gave me.'[11]

For fifteen years Walpole maintained his power against the assaults of his enemies. As Horace Walpole observes, exaggerat-

---

[8] *The Works of Lord Bolingbroke*, I (Philadelphia, 1841), pp. 332–3.

[9] Quoted by Petrie in *Bolingbroke* (London, 1937), p. 310.

[10] William Coxe, *Memoirs of the Life and Administration of Sir Robert Walpole*, II (London, 1798), p. 339.

[11] Coxe, II, 338.

ing his father's equanimity but not the security of his control, 'Craftsman, pamphlets, libels, combinations, were showered on or employed for years against the Prime Minister, without shaking his power or ruffling his temper.'[12] Yet with the passage of time Walpole's popularity inevitably declined and the ranks of his enemies grew. As he had always known, Bolingbroke was a formidable opponent. 'I see you', Swift had written to Bolingbroke in 1729, 'as much esteemed, as much beloved, as much dreaded, and perhaps more (though it be almost impossible) than e'er you were in your highest exaltation.'[13] In the struggle over the Excise Bill in 1733 Walpole experienced his first serious setback, and he was able to maintain himself at the head of affairs chiefly because he managed to hold the support of the Court and because the only real alternative to Walpole, a Bolingbroke ministry, could not command the support of all the factions which made up the Opposition. Nevertheless, the popular agitation against the Excise manifested passions far out of proportion to the argument over the Bill itself, and, in fact, constituted a national demonstration against the régime.[14]

In attacking Walpole's foreign policy the Opposition stressed his uncertain and pusillanimous handling of relations with Spain. The question of Gibraltar had not been satisfactorily settled, and, furthermore, Spanish pirates attacked British shipping with impunity. Another issue was the Government's failure to see that France destroyed the fortifications of the port of Dunkirk, as provided for by treaty. Bolingbroke's secretary, Brinsden, made a personal visit to the port, and, basing its attack on his account, the Opposition made it appear that France, like Spain, could safely ignore British interests. Domestically, the principal theme of the Opposition was the subservience of Parliament to the administration. Charges of bribery and peculation were hurled, with justice, at the Government. The Commons passed the Pension Bill, which disabled pensioners and office-holders from sitting as Members of Parliament, and so diminished the leverage of the administration. Though the

---

[12] Horace Walpole, *Reminiscences of the Reign of George II* (Boston, 1820), p. 17.

[13] *The Correspondence of Alexander Pope*, III, p. 63.

[14] For the growth of the opposition to Walpole, see Charles B. Realey, *The Early Opposition of Sir Robert Walpole* (Kansas, 1932), and J. H. Plumb, *Sir Robert Walpole*, II. Coxe, II, pp. 320 ff., is also valuable.

Bill was rejected by the Lords, it nevertheless was a popular measure, and its rejection caused a further decline in Walpole's popularity. In Plumb's vivid phrase, 'an honest placeman, as far as the public was concerned, was a figure of fantasy as remarkable and rare as the unicorn or the phoenix'.[15] And, of course, Walpole himself, red-faced and corpulent, with his unfaithful wife and his homely mistress, spending huge sums of money of mysterious origin on his collection of paintings; the inept Horatio Walpole, whose sole qualification for his diplomatic post was his undeviating loyalty to the régime, and who, sneered at by the sophisticates in the capitals of Europe, seemed the perfect symbol of Walpole's foreign policy; the pathetic Newcastle, writing and rewriting his endless despatches, a hopeless gull before the intricacies of Continental politics—all these provided targets of the most inviting sort for the wits and satirists, pamphleteers and polemicists, whom Bolingbroke gathered about him at Dawley.[16]

Ironically enough, Bolingbroke, who had worked so long to form an effective and united Opposition, was excluded from the political struggles which actually did bring about the fall of Walpole. As it turned out, the climax of Bolingbroke's efforts in behalf of the Opposition came in 1734. Walpole's defeat in the struggle over the Excise Bill, his growing unpopularity, the gains made by the Opposition in the election of 1734, had raised the hopes of all who wished to see him destroyed. At last, it began to seem, the 'great man' and his powerful machine might be decisively defeated. Nevertheless, despite the growing numbers and increased confidence of Walpole's enemies, there were few issues on which they all could agree. When Bromley, supported by Wyndham, moved the repeal of the Septennial Act, a Tory move designed to bring about more frequent elections and so make Parliament more responsive to public opinion, Pulteney complained that Wyndham was too much the creature of Bolingbroke. The Septennial Act, passed upon the accession of George I to insure the Government against popular resentment, was too much of a Whig measure for even opposition Whigs to desire its repeal. The Opposition thus split along Whig and Tory lines, a situation Walpole was quick to exploit. When

[15] J. H. Plumb, *Sir Robert Walpole*, II, p. 150.
[16] Ibid., p. 131.

Wyndham, supporting repeal, delivered a speech probably composed by Bolingbroke, Walpole, ignoring Wyndham, answered with a savagely eloquent attack on Bolingbroke himself. The two speeches, Wyndham's and Walpole's, epitomise the conflict itself, and go far toward defining the reasons for Bolingbroke's sudden withdrawl from Opposition politics in 1735. Wyndham argued for repeal by stating the Opposition's case against Walpole:

> . . . Let us suppose a gentleman at the head of the administration, whose only safety depends upon corrupting the members of this House. This may now be only a supposition, but it is certainly such a one as may happen; and, if ever it should, let us see if such a Minister might not promise himself more success in a septennial than he could in a triennial Parliament, It is an old maxim that every man has his price, if you can but come up to it. This, I hope, does not hold true of every man, but I am afraid it too generally holds true . . . Let us then suppose, sir, a man abandoned to all notions of virtue and honour, of no great family, and but a mean fortune, raised to the Chief Minister of State by the concurrence of many whimsical events. . . . Suppose him next possessed of great wealth, the plunder of the nation, with a Parliament of his own choosing, most of their seats purchased, and their votes bought at the expense of the public treasure. In such a Parliament let us suppose attempts made to enquire into his conduct, or to relieve the nation from the distress he has brought upon it; and when lights proper for attaining these ends are called for . . . suppose, then, these lights refused . . . Upon this scandalous victory let us suppose this Chief Minister pluming himself in defiance because he has got a Parliament like a packed jury, ready to acquit him of all adventures. Let us further suppose him arrived to that degree of arrogance and insolence as to domineer over all the men of ancient families, all the men of sense, fortune, or figure in the nation, and as he has no virtue of his own, ridiculing it in others, and endeavouring to destroy or corrupt it in all . . . I am still not prophesying, sir, I am only supposing . . .[17]

Wyndham's speech was a brilliant one, recapitulating all the familiar charges against Walpole, and appealing, above party, to men's patriotism; but Walpole's reply reached heights of

---

[17] *The Parliamentary History of England*, IX (London, 1811), pp. 460–6.

invective equal to, perhaps even superior to, Wyndham's. He shrewdly attacked the Opposition at its weakest point, recalling in lurid terms the checkered political career of its real leader, Bolingbroke:

. . . But now, sir, let me too suppose, and the House being cleared, I am sure no person that hears me can come within the description of the person I am to suppose. Let us suppose in this, or some other unfortunate country, an anti-Minister, who thinks himself a person of so great and extensive parts, and of so many eloquent qualifications, that he looks upon himself as the only person in the kingdom capable to conduct the public affairs of the nation, and therefore christens every other administration by the name of Blunderer. Suppose this fine gentleman to have gained over to his party some persons really of fine parts, of ancient families, and of great fortunes, and others, of desperate views arising from disappointed and malicious hearts, all these gentlemen, with respect to their political behaviour, moved by him and by him solely, all they say either in private or public being only a repetition of the words he has put into their mouths and a spitting out of that venom which he has infused into them. And yet we may suppose this leader not really liked by any, even of those who so blindly follow him, and hated by all the rest of mankind. We will suppose this anti-Minister to be in a country where he really ought not to be, and where he could not have been but by an effect of too much goodness and mercy, yet endeavouring with all his might and all his art to destroy the fountain from whence that mercy flowed. In that country suppose him continually contracting friendships and familiarities with ambassadors of those princes who at the time happen to be most at enmity with his own . . . Let us suppose this anti-Minister to have travelled, and at every court where he was, thinking himself the greatest Minister, and making it his trade to betray the secrets of every court where he had been before; void of all faith, or honour, and betraying every master he ever served. I could carry my suppositions a great deal further; and I may say now I mean no person now in being; but if we can suppose such a one, can there by imagined a greater disgrace to human nature than such a wretch as this?[18]

To the growing and increasingly confident Opposition, which drew much of its strength from disaffected Whigs like Pulteney,

[18] Ibid., pp. 471–2.

Chesterfield, and their followers, Bolingbroke must have seemed more and more of a liability. His role in Queen Anne's ministry, his Jacobite intrigues in 1715, made him vulnerable to the kind of attack Walpole had been able to make upon him. And so, ironically, as the Opposition became more powerful, as it sensed the possibility of actually assuming power, Bolingbroke became more dispensable. Bolingbroke himself recognised the political reality. As he wrote to Wyndham, Pulteney thought his 'very name and presence in England did hurt' to the cause of the Opposition.[19] In the summer of 1735, accordingly, Bolingbroke retired to France, arriving on 23 June, after a rough journey by land and sea, at his chateau, Chantelou. The largest establishment he ever occupied, Chantelou was located at Touraine, the same region as La Source. He had decided, as he wrote to Wyndham, never to buy land again, 'no, not a burying place', and so he merely rented Chantelou, meanwhile selling La Source and planning the sale of Dawley. After he reached France he took account of his political fortunes in a letter to Wyndham: 'You are grown to be a formidable minority within doors, and you have a great majority without. I am still the same proscribed man, surrounded with difficulties, exposed to mortifications, and unable to take any share in the service but that which I have taken hitherto, and which, I think, you would persuade me to take in the present state of things. My part is over, and he who remains on the stage after his part is over deserves to be hissed off . . .'[20]

Convinced, at least for the time being, that political power would not again be his, Bolingbroke turned now from political action to reflection upon the principles which governed it, turned, that is, to the literary composition for which his mastery of English prose style so well suited him. As Lord Orrery, alluding to Bolingbroke's literary ability, remarked to Swift in 1741, 'Lord Bolingbroke lives in France; posterity, it is to be hoped, will be the better for his retirement.'[21] A garden pavilion was his favourite place for composition, and so he had one constructed there, and also at the abbey at Sens, where his wife

---

[19] Coxe, II, p. 523.

[20] Walter Sichel, *Bolingbroke and His Times*, II (New York, 1902), p. 311.

[21] *The Correspondence of Jonathan Swift*, ed. F. Elrington Ball (London, 1910–14), p. 178.

periodically convalesced. When he was not writing he hunted, or else worked in his gardens.

Bolingbroke was preparing at this time a philosophical epistle for Pope, and planning to secure material from the Duchess of Marlborough for a history he never, finally, wrote. In January 1736 he gave to his brother-in-law Robert Knight two packets, one for Lord Bathurst, the other for Lord Cornbury. To Bathurst he sent *The True Use of Retirement and Study*; to Cornbury, *On the Study and Use of History*; and later that year he sent to Cornbury the *Letter on the Spirit of Patriotism*, in which he begins to explore some of the themes that he would treat more fully in *The Idea of a Patriot King*.

Meanwhile, in England, during these initial months of Bolingbroke's withdrawal, the emergence of the presumptive heir to the throne, Prince Frederick, was providing a new rallying-point for the Opposition. The various groups which made up the Opposition had lacked a programme on which they could agree and a leader who could serve as a symbol for their cause. Bolingbroke was too much identified with the Tory programme under Anne to enlist the support of the dissident Whigs; his relations with James, embittered as they were, made him unacceptable to the Jacobites. Yet a truly national figure became available in 1733 when Frederick Louis, Prince of Wales, emerged as an independent political force.[22] The eldest son of George II and Queen Caroline, Frederick did not arrive in England until he was 21, yet for some time before that there had been a noticeable coolness between the Prince and his father the King. Frederick had loved with adolescent intensity one Sophia Dorothea Wilhelmina, a Princess of Prussia, and although George had set himself against the match, young Frederick, showing the spirit of independence which later so embittered his relations with the King, had schemed to marry her in private. Just in time, from the King's point of view, the marriage was forestalled by the intervention of the British Ambassador. The relations of father and son were never again the same. When Frederick finally came to England their atti-

[22] For the career of Prince Frederick, see J. H. Plumb, *The First Four Georges* (London, 1956); Walter Sichel, *Bolingbroke and His Times*, II (New York, 1902), pp. 215–315; Horace Walpole's *Reminiscences*, op. cit.; and *The Dictionary of National Biography*.

tude toward one another caused whispers at Court. The breach rapidly widened, becoming the scandal of the reign. As his crony Bubb Doddington guided him into increasing truc- ulence, Frederick became something of a celebrity, even a popular hero, by trying in various ways to outshine his father, an endeavour in which success was by no means difficult. The young Prince seemed amiable, even dashing, and, when one thought of his father, graceful and intelligent. During the early thirties he figured in the famous Tweedledum-Tweedledee controversy, in which, opposing his sister, the friend and patroness of Handel, whose operas were being performed at the theatre in Haymarket, Prince Frederick supported the rival composer Buoncini, whose works were applauded in Lincoln's Inn Fields, and the rivalry had the attention of the fashionable world for a season. Soon, however, Frederick began to cultivate more serious antagonisms. By 1733 he was associating purpose- fully with Opposition politicians, by 1734 insisting upon mar- riage and a separate establishment. In 1735, getting his way, he married Princess Augusta of Saxe-Gotha, but the King, never adept at conciliation, still refused him the allowance that many, indeed the public at large, regarded as his due. The Prince appealed to Parliament. His requests were rejected by both Houses. The Prince retaliated by neglecting to tell the King and Queen of his wife's pregnancy. Finally, when Augusta was almost in labour, he suddenly fled with her in the middle of the night from Hampton Court, where his parents were, to St. James's Palace, though no preparations had been made there to care for the Princess. In fact, the only woman in attendance at St. James's was Lady Hamilton, reputed to be the Prince's mistress. The reason for this extraordinary flight was believed to be his hatred for the King and Queen. He did not want them present at the birth of his child. When the King ordered him out of St. James's Palace he removed to Kew and then to Norfolk House. King George quite characteristically made matters worse, if that were possible, by sending copies of his correspondence with Frederick to British Ambassadors abroad, and, even worse, to foreign representatives in England, demand- ing that they avoid visiting the Prince, 'a thing that would be disagreeable to his majesty'.

The Prince's new establishment at Norfolk House became the

gathering place for the Opposition, and such political leaders as Wyndham, Pulteney, Chesterfield, Carteret, and Cobham assembled there. As the centre of this group the Prince commanded a growing power. He could, in addition, influence elections in his Duchy, Cornwall, and he could hold out to young politicians, such as William Pitt, who were willing to wait in the wings, the prospect of future office. From the point of view of the Opposition, the Prince was valuable in symbolic ways. He was a Hanoverian, and so Walpole could no longer charge that all his opponents were Jacobites at heart. What is more, it seemed certain in 1737 that Frederick, at 30, represented the future, in contrast to the King, who was 54, and Walpole, who was 61.

Both King George and his Queen detested their eldest son, and though they usually seemed phlegmatically German, their expressions regarding Frederick glow with a passion long cultivated.[23] 'If I was to see him in Hell,' said Caroline, 'I should feel no more for him than I should for any other rogue that ever went there.' According to Lord Harvey, Caroline also spoke of her son in these terms: 'My dear firstborn is the greatest ass, and the greatest liar, and the greatest canaille, and the greatest beast in the whole world, and I most heartily wish he was out of it.' But in spite of such maternal sentiments, the King regarded her as excessively biased in the Prince's favour and likely to judge his character too favourably—for he viewed the Prince as 'a monster and the greatest villain that ever was born'. When Frederick, for his part, heard of his mother's impending death, he remarked: 'Well, now we shall have some good news; she cannot hold out much longer.' Caroline continued the feud to the end, refusing, though on her death-bed, to see her son, and announcing that his own request to see her was a piece of crass hypocrisy. Even when she was dying one of her last thoughts was that by some fluke the Prince might inherit part of her property, and she therefore insisted upon sending for Lord Chancellor Hardwicke, who assured her that her property was entirely beyond her son's reach.

The vindictiveness with which the King, never popular, treated the Prince aroused sympathy for Frederick among the

[23] This account of Frederick's embittered relations with George and Caroline follows J. H. Plumb, *The First Four Georges* (New York, 1957), pp. 83–86.

people. He became a kind of popular hero. To cheer for Frederick as he passed was a way of expressing contempt for George and Walpole. The growing popularity of Frederick thus increased the hope of ultimate success among the leaders of the Opposition.

Bolingbroke seems to have been oblivious to these events, and mainly concerned with his rural pursuits. In the spring of 1736 ill health made him change his French residence, and this may be an indication that he was feeling restless in spirit. 'I rise,' he wrote to Wyndham in 1736, 'and read, or write, or walk about. I give full employment to this fluttering activity of spirits. When I cannot sleep as I would, I take it as I can; and like my brother animals, I recover by snatches in the day what I lost in the night.'24 Accordingly, in May of that year he moved his household to Argeville, near the forest of Fontaine-bleau, which was to be his home for six years. His health improved with exercise. 'You and I use too little exercise,' he had written to Wyndham. 'I am resolved to turn poacher . . .' And so at Argeville hunting became a passion with him. He studied the breeding of horses and dogs, which he imported for the purpose, and he hunted wolves and wild boar. Pope describes his life there in a letter to Swift: 'His plan of life is now a very agreeable one in the finest country in France, divided between study and exercise; for he still reads or writes five or six hours a day, and generally hunts twice a week. He has the whole forest of Fontainebleau at his command, with the King's stables, dogs, etc., his lady's son-in-law being governor of that place. She resides part of the year with my lord, at a large house they have hired; and the rest with her daughter, who is abbess of a royal convent in the neighbourhood.'25 Bolingbroke himself describes his life at Argeville in a letter of March 1738 to his brother-in-law: 'As I was a farmer in England, I am a hunts-man in France, and am less diverted from the latter than I was from the former. The love of hunting, which returned strongly upon me, is confirmed by the health that exercise gives me; and I, who could never go out to take a walk, should sit with a few books and fewer friends if the cry of dogs and sound of horns did not draw me abroad.' He even takes time to praise his dogs:

24 Sichel, II, p. 362.
25 *The Correspondence of Alexander Pope*, IV, pp. 176-7.

'They are brave hounds, and I would tell you stories of their prowess, especially of one of them, the lightest coloured, that would please you if you was a sportsman.'[26]

Despite his ostensible unconcern for English politics, however, he kept abreast of affairs through his correspondence with Sir William Wyndham, and continued to urge a consistent pro- gramme of opposition to Walpole, 'a scheme of conduct wisely formed, and concerted among all those that stand in opposition to the present administration'.[27] And he reiterated his convic- tion that, behind the façade of the traditional constitutional forms, the oligarchy was subverting the Constitution itself: 'Whenever will prevails constantly and without control or account, the will of a prince or the will of a minister, whatever forms are preserved, tyranny is established.'[28] The insight that the effect of government might change despite the maintenance of outward forms was one that he soon would expand upon in *The Idea of a Patriot King*. He urged, furthermore, that Prince Frederick be used as a lever to topple Walpole from power. The Prince's prudence and dignity, dutifulness and moderation, were not enough, he wrote to Wyndham, and indeed were likely to 'keep him where he is, you where you are, and Walpole where he is', but that Walpole 'would think the circumstances much more unpleasant and have more disquietude about future events, if the prince was at this time retired to Southampton House; for instance, if he lived there, with all the economy of a private nobleman, and was surrounded with friends that might adorn the court of a prince'.[29]

In view of this advice, it is odd to find Bolingbroke a few months later, in October 1737, failing to grasp the importance of Frederick's break with his father, and deprecating it to Wyndham. One can only suppose that, removed from affairs as he was, he did not have an accurate sense of the political climate in London:

I am at a loss to find the plausibility or the popularity of the present rupture. He hurries his wife from Court when she is upon the point of being delivered of her first child. His father

[26] British Museum MSS. 34196.
[27] Coxe, II, p. 479.
[28] Coxe, II, p. 479.
[29] Coxe, II, p. 480.

sweels, struts, and storms. He confesses his rashness, and asks pardon in the terms of one who owns himself in the wrong. Besides that all seems to me boyish, it is purely domestic, and there is nothing, as far as I can discern, to interest the public in the cause of his Royal Highness.[30]

How mistaken he was Bolingbroke discovered when he crossed the Channel in June of the following year. He sold Dawley for £26,000, and visited old friends, including Pope, who had grown friendly with Warburton, chaplain to Prince Frederick. And now, no doubt because of such associations, Bolingbroke found that once again he desired to play an active role in British politics. As he wrote to Marchmont after returning to France, 'Your fire revived the dying embers of mine . . . I returned to my hermitage not only with a concern for my country, which will accompany me everywhere, but with a mind bent on endeavours to be of utility even there.'[31]

It was in this mood that he composed, in the later part of 1738, *The Idea of a Patriot King*. Though it was not published until eleven years later, its ideas, through Bolingbroke's conversation, had by then long been familiar at the Patriot Court, and the book itself, privately printed by Pope, had circulated among the wits and politicians there. Mable H. Cable has shown that Bolingbroke's ideas were taken up and versified by the poets that Frederick had gathered to his cause on the advice of Pitt and Lyttelton, among them Thomson, Mallet, Brooke, and Glover.[32] No doubt Bolingbroke wrote *The Idea of a Patriot King* with the intention of attracting the attention of Frederick, and perhaps even in the hope of effecting his own return to leadership of the Opposition. If so, it failed in this purpose. The Opposition might make use of Bolingbroke's ideas, but it no longer needed his leadership, and now acted independently of him. In 1739, for example, contravening Bolingbroke's advice, the so-called Patriots marched one by one out of the House during a debate over policy toward Spain. Bolingbroke had considered that such a gesture was ineffective, a way of avoid-

[30] Coxe, II, p. 480.
[31] Marchmont Papers, II, 178: quoted in Sichel, II, p. 362.
[32] Mable H. Cable, 'The Idea of a Patriot King in the Propaganda of the Opposition to Walpole, 1735–1739', *Philological Quarterly*, XVIII (1939), pp. 119–30.

ing a fight rather than pressing it. What is more, Bolingbroke's friends were dying or passing from influence, and younger men, long excluded from power by Walpole, were moving to the centre of the stage. Sir William Wyndham died suddenly in 1740. He had long been Bolingbroke's confidant, and the spokesman for his views in Parliament. 'What a star has our minister!' exclaimed Bolingbroke. 'Wyndham dead, Marchmont disabled! The loss of Marchmont and Wyndham to our country. "*Multis fortunae vulneribus percussus, huic uni se imparem sensit.*" '[33] The political milieu in which Bolingbroke had been so effective no longer really existed, and a new spirit was stirring in the country. 'There was steadily growing a reaction,' as Winston Churchill says, 'both in the country and in the House of Commons, to the interminable monopoly of power by this tough, unsentimental Norfolk squire, with his head for figures and his horror of talent, keeping the country quiet, and, though it was only an incident, feathering his own nest . . . The country was bored. It rejected a squalid, peaceful prosperity. Trade figures swelled. Still the country was dissatisfied . . . All that was keen and adventurous in the English character writhed under this sordid, sleepy government.'[34] *The Craftsman*, the works of the satirists, poems like Thomson's *Liberty* and Glover's *Leonidas*, obscure pamphlets emanating from Grub Street—all had done their work. Bolingbroke could have heard his own slogans repeated everywhere, protesting corrupt ministers and Royal indifference, placemen, dishonourable compromises, septennial Parliaments, and blundering commercial policies. There were riots in London. Prince Frederick, cheered by the opponents of the Government, made appearances all over the city. As his régime tottered toward its fall in February 1742, Walpole sat for hours, alone and silent, at his house in Downing Street.[35] Yet even under such circumstances as these, and though Bolingbroke had worked to bring them about and prepare the national mood, the country was not to turn to him, ageing as he was and tarnished by the issues and intrigues of other reigns. After Walpole's fall, over the issue of war with

[33] Marchmont Papers, II, p. 225: quoted in Sichel, II, pp. 362–3.
[34] Winston Churchill, *The Age of Revolution*, Vol. III of *A History of the English Speaking Peoples* (New York, 1957), pp. 118–19.
[35] Ibid., p. 122.

Spain, the Government at Whitehall was managed by Henry Pelham and his brother, the Duke of Newcastle, whose enormous wealth and consequent electoral influence enabled them to control the House of Commons. In Bolingbroke's view, the long campaign of the Opposition had been betrayed. None of the measures that had been the centre of the Opposition programme were to be put into effect: in fact, the country would wait until the next century for Parliamentary reform. In Bolingbroke's opinion, the change of ministry was 'a farce'. People had expected 'a change of men, and, with them, a change of measures. How have all these expectations been answered? Not in one single point.' The fight against Walpole, which he had considered one of principle, seemed to him now to have been waged by many for purely selfish ends—'not a struggle for liberty, but places'.[36] Nothing was to be done about the Septennial Act, or about restoring the independence of Parliament by limiting the number of placemen. 'Some persons', he wrote to Marchmont, 'meant that the opposition should serve as their scaffolding, nothing else.'[37] To make matters worse, England plunged into an inept war with Spain. Bolingbroke had long attacked Walpole's passivity toward Spain, but had argued, probably correctly, that earlier resistance to Spanish insults and piracy would have made war unnecessary.

During the last decades of his life Bolingbroke was a spectator, as far as politics was concerned, though he maintained his close interest in foreign affairs, and forwarded to his friend Hardwicke, the Lord Chancellor, what information he could gather about the French Court through his personal contacts there. His philosophical reflections occupied him as well, and he revised the notes on theology that he had written for Pope's benefit. He was aware, though, that the temper of the culture was changing, and that it would be less receptive than it once had been to his urbane scepticism. A symptom of this change was the growing popularity of George Whitefield's evangelical preaching. In a letter to Marchmont, written in November 1748, Bolingbroke describes with dry humour how even Chesterfield, that epitome of worldly cynicism, had been moved by this great preacher:

[36] British Museum MSS. 37994: letter to Marchmont, 1 November 1748.
[37] Ibid.

I hope you heard from me by myself as well as of me by Mr. Whitefield, for I answered your Lordship's precedent letters. This apostolical person preached some time ago at Lady Huntingdon's, and I should have been anxious to hear him. Nothing kept me from going but an imagination that there was to be a select auditory. That saint, our friend Chesterfield, was there and I heard from him an extream good account of the sermon. He came away with much desire to be one of the Temples of God. If he grows such, or can persuade himself of it, he may own very safely under so good a Christian as our present majesty that he is a *Theophorus*; though that contention cost the blessed martyr Ignatius dear when Trajan sent him to the lions.[38]

By 1749, when *The Idea of a Patriot King* finally was published, Bolingbroke's turbulent career was nearing its end. Most of his friends and enemies had already passed from the scene; Pope and Swift, Gay, Wyndham, and the Duchess of Marlborough were all dead. Sir Robert Walpole had died as Earl of Orford in 1745. It is very likely that Bolingbroke felt the loss of his great antagonist as sharply as that of his closest allies, for he had defined his political position in polemical opposition to the power of the Norfolk squire. And in fact, Walpole's death served to mark the end of Bolingbroke's era as much as did the death of Pope. The Pelhams, the Grenvilleites, were the ascendant forces in politics, and William Pitt was emerging—unpredictable, paranoid, but eloquent—as a power in national politics. Indeed, children were then being born who would witness the accession of Victoria. Under Pitt, England would be launched on its career of global empire, an idea that would have been as strange to Walpole as to Bolingbroke, both of whom, in different ways, focused inward in their politics.

The death of Bolingbroke's father, Old Frumps, the Restoration rake, incredibly delayed, occurred at last in April 1742, and Battersea Manor, the family seat and the place of his birth sixty years before, passed into Bolingbroke's hands. 'I go into my own country', he wrote in 1744, 'as if I went into a strange country, and shall inhabit my own house as if I lodged in an inn.' Battersea was a splendid manor house, with its grand staircase, wainscoted halls, fluted columns, and cedar-panelled

[38] Ibid.

study, and it stood close by Battersea Church on the south side of the Thames, surrounded by gardens and pleasant fields. Living quietly, Bolingbroke kept in touch with political affairs, though he must have seemed the ghost of another era to the young politicians who visited him. For his own part, Bolingbroke considered the most prominent of them, William Pitt, 'extremely supercilious'. Often in ill health, his thoughts were most often on the past. 'I look often back with regret,' he wrote to Marchmont in 1747, 'and dare not look forward at all. I recall often to mind what my friend Arbuthnot said to me just before he died, that I should live to see what he was happy enough to avoid seeing by dying before me.'[39]

Prince Frederick, by an odd coincidence, lived only until 1751, the year in which Bolingbroke also died, and the last years of the Prince's life were marked by futility, pathos, and farce, strangely commingled. For a time, after the fall of Walpole, he was partially reconciled to the King, but he broke with him again when George refused to increase his allowance. During the Jacobite rebellion of 1745 Frederick longed to lead the Royal armies, but was refused the command, and subsequently, it was said, he was instrumental in bringing about the release of Flora MacDonald after her assistance to the escape of Prince Charles. Despite the hopes of the Opposition, Frederick was destined never to succeed to the throne. He passed his time gambling, he patronised literature; according to Horace Walpole, 'the chief passion of the Prince was women; but, like the rest of his race, beauty was not a necessary ingredient'. He had a bastard, Cornwall Fitz-Frederick, by Anne Vane, and a certain absurdity clings even to his death, widely mourned though he was, which was brought about, quite suddenly, in March 1751, by the bursting of an abscess formed by a blow from a tennis ball.

Despite his failing health, Bolingbroke remained intellectually vigorous. In the spring of 1751 he was asked by Dr. Heberden to read over some posthumous theological manuscripts of Conyers Middleton, and after studying them he recommended that the essays on the Bible be published 'after some polishing'. He found essay No. Three 'a very good one, on the

[39] Ibid.

dispute between St. Peter and St. Paul', and says No. Five 'contains a very accurate search into ecclesiastical antiquity . . . and the great principle he insists upon to be the sole principle upon which the consistency of the Gospels and their authority can be supported [seems] sufficiently proved'.[40] Bolingbroke's own religious views have been the subject of dispute, and much depends upon the weight given to his various statements within the context in which they occur. Yet after a careful reading of his works, manuscripts, and correspondence, the following conclusion seems to me the most defensible. He believed in what he called a Supreme Being, and in the operation of general, absolute moral laws derived from that Supreme Being. The very strength of his belief in those general laws, however, made him sceptical in regard to what has been called the 'scandal of particularity'—the idea that the Supreme Being could reveal himself in a particular place and at a particular time. As regards particular providence he was equally sceptical: he regarded this as 'a matter of opinion'.

During the summer of 1751 a 'humour' on Bolingbroke's face became malignant. The agonies it caused were heightened by the ministrations of a quack to whom he applied for treatment. 'I am at present', he wrote in August—and the handwriting in the manuscript makes it clear that he is dictating—'under a painful and troublesome cure for a cancer in my face. The remedy has succeeded in a multitude of cases which I have examined and verified. I should be even more unfortunate than it belongs to me to be, if it failed in my case alone. It makes it impossible for me to stir from home, or to see anybody at home except doctors, surgeons, and those with whom I am entirely intimate.'[41] Early in December, Chesterfield visited him for the last time, finding him in great pain. When they parted, according to Chesterfield, Bolingbroke said to him, 'God who placed me here will do what He pleases with me hereafter, and He knows best what to do.' A few days later he lost consciousness, and, surviving his wife by less than nine months, died on 12 December in the house where he had been born. On 18 December he was buried beside her in the family vault of Battersea Church, his epitaph, like hers, composed by himself:

[40] British Museum MSS. 34196.
[41] Ibid.

Here lyes
HENRY ST. JOHN
In the days of Queen Anne
Secretary at War, Secretary of State, and Viscount Bolingbroke;
In the days of King George the First and King George the Second,
Something more and better.
His attachment to Queen Anne
Exposed him to a long and severe prosecution:
He bore it with firmness of mind.
He passed the latter part of his life at home,
The enemy of no national party
The friend of no faction;
Distinguished under a cloud of proscription
Which had not been entirely taken off
By zeal to maintain the Liberty
And to restore the ancient Prosperity
Of Great Britain.

V

"THE IDEA OF A PATRIOT KING" AND THE RATIONAL BASIS OF MONARCHY

As we have seen, *The Idea of a Patriot King* was, in at least one of its aspects, a topical work. Written in 1738, when Prince Frederick was emerging as a rallying-point for the various groups that made up the Opposition, it was calculated to impress and flatter him. Bolingbroke had been shunted aside by Pulteney and the other Opposition Whigs, who viewed him as a liability. Nevertheless, if he could manage to ingratiate himself with the heir to the throne, so it must have seemed to him, he might once again wield the power that had slipped from him. Thus, like Machiavelli's *The Prince*, a book with which it has the closest of intellectual relationships, *The Idea of a Patriot King* reflected the hopes, fated to frustration, of a defeated politician.

The reference of Bolingbroke's book to a particular political situation is a feature it has in common with the manuals of many and perhaps most writers *de regimine principum*.[1] However,

---

[1] Hoccleve devoted half of his work to his own affairs, and perhaps wished the liberality which he urged upon the King to include a pension for the poet. Giraldus Cambrensis devoted the second and third parts of his work to a fierce attack upon Henry II, and the first part embodies a norm of virtuous conduct for rulers, against which Henry may be measured. Gilbert of Tournai and Vincent of Beauvais wrote with one eye on Louis IX, and Egidio Colonna, writing for Philip the Fair, modified his Aristotelianism to suit the purposes of the French monarchy. Erasmus, perhaps Bolingbroke's most notable predecessor in the genre, if we except Machiavelli, addressed Prince Charles, and devoted the chapter *de bello suscipiendo*, which in the genre was customarily devoted to a discussion of military techniques, to a denunciation of war—a central theme of Erasmus's work and one particularly

again like *The Prince*, *The Idea of a Patriot King* was written with posterity in mind. After all, both Frederick and Lorenzo were likely to prove unequal to the tasks required of them. The two manuals, therefore, were also meant to epitomise their authors' thought on ethics and politics. No less than *The Prince* was *The Idea of a Patriot King* intended to be a work of political science, its principal object as such being the defence of the humanist values which, in Bolingbroke's view, Machiavelli had attacked. He wished to construct an exemplary image of the monarch, relevant to his own time, which might be imitated as had the exemplary figures of classical and Renaissance tradition. 'When Tully informs us', observed Bolingbroke in *On the Study and Use of History*,

> that the first Scipio Africanus had always in his hands the works of Xenophon, he advances nothing but what is probable and reasonable. To say nothing of the retreat of the ten-thousand, nor of other parts of Xenophon's writings; the images of virtue, represented in that admirable picture the Cyropaedia, were proper to entertain a soul that was fraught with virtue, and Cyrus was worthy to be imitated by Scipio.[2]

Bolingbroke thinks that stories of an historical sort, whether or not they are entirely true, have a morally inspiring effect. He cannot suppose that doubts concerning credibility have ever prevented any 'man of candour' from applying examples he has found in history to the judgment of the present, and he wonders rhetorically whether such a man 'has not been touched with reverence and admiration, at the virtue and wisdom of some men and of some ages; and whether he has not felt indignation and contempt for others? Whether Epaminondas or Phocion, for instance, the Decii, or the Scipio, have not raised in his mind a flame of public spirit and private virtue? and whether he has not shuddered with horror at the prescriptions of Marius and Sylla. . . .'[3] As a humanist, Bolingbroke is

---

[2] *The Works of Lord Bolingbroke*, II (Philadelphia, 1841), p. 180.
[3] Ibid., p. 219.

---

appropriate to his own time. Like Bolingbroke and Machiavelli, these writers did not hesitate to apply their generalisations to contemporary problems, and they moved easily between general rule and particular instance.

always concerned to stress the educational function of literature. The humanist attitude toward learning could scarcely be stated less equivocally than in these words of Bolingbroke: 'we ought to apply, and, the shortness of human life considered, to confine ourselves almost entirely in our study of history, to such histories as have an immediate relation to our professions, to our rank and situation in the society to which we belong'.[4] *The Idea of a Patriot King*, accordingly, reflects this conception of the function of literature. Bolingbroke contends that his conception of a ruler will embody rational ethical principle and will, if imitated, help to counteract the effect of the alternative image constructed by Machiavelli.

As has already been shown, earlier humanist writers had viewed the character of the ruler and of the governing class as the central concern of political philosophy. Some thousand books, or important sections of books, had been devoted to teaching the ruler to function in a way that would make him a blessing rather than a curse, beloved rather than hated.[5] When Machiavelli wrote *The Prince*, it is evident, he supposed that the novel quality of his teaching would be immediately understood because so many other books had been written on the subject: 'I know that many have written on this,' he says.[6] The content of such volumes, as developed during the evolution of this tradition, had become more or less standardised. The headings used by Vincent of Beauvais, for example, in his *De morali principis institutione*, correspond in most cases to sections in the manuals of Erasmus, Machiavelli, and Bolingbroke. In fact, the chapter headings which Pope introduced into Bolingbroke's manual in the privately printed 1740 edition serve to emphasise the relationship of the book to the *de regimine* tradition. The order in which the various topics are taken up corresponds, generally speaking, to that of *The Prince* and to other manuals

---

[4] Ibid., p. 230.

[5] Allen H. Gilbert, *Machiavelli's Prince and Its Forerunners* (Durham, 1938), p. 3.

[6] *The Prince*, Ch. XV. In the case of Machiavelli, citation of the chapter which is the source of the quotation seems a sufficient guide for reference. This has the advantage of permitting the reader to use any edition of Machiavelli at his disposal. The most-often cited Italian edition of Machiavelli's *Opere* was edited by F. Flora and C. Cordie (Milan, 1949–50). The translations of Machiavelli used in this essay come from *The Prince and the Discourses*, trans. Luigi Pricci, rev. E. R. P. Vincent (New York, 1940).

of the same sort.[7] Machiavelli, however, seems to have thought

[7] Here are the chapter headings in the 1740 edition of *The Idea of a Patriot King*: Ch. I: 1. What are the duties of Kings from the nature of their institution? 2. The source of the opinions concerning the divine right and absolute power of Kings. Ch. II: 1. What are the duties of subjects, from the constitution of human nature and law of society? 2. The true right of Kings and obedience of subjects. 3. Which is best, hereditary monarchy, or elective? 4. A limited monarchy the best form of government, and hereditary the best monarchy. Ch. III: 1. The peculiar advantage of a limited monarchy over all other forms of government. 2. The absurdity of supposing arbitrary power essential to monarchy. 3. The nature of such limitations as are consistent with monarchy. 4. Objections against limitations answered. Ch. IV: 1. That such limitations will be no restraints to a prince who is truly a patriot. 2. How it happens that so few princes are patriots. 3. A digression. What ought to be the conduct of those about a prince, and what is the duty of all who approach him? Ch. V: 1. What the situations will be of a prince who during a bad reign gives hopes of a good one. His advantages both before, and after his accession. 2. The opinion of Machiavel on this point. Ch. VI: 1. What will be the views, pursuant to the former principles, of a patriot King? 2. That those principles and views will be the same, whether he be hereditary or elective. Ch. VII: 1. What will be the conduct of a patriot King, in order to restore a free Constitution? 2. How by the contrary conduct, a bad or weak prince is capable of destroying one. 3. But that a good King is really sufficient to this task. 4. The ability of a patriot King to restore a free Constitution. Ch. VIII: 1. A previous observation. 2. The measures a patriot King will take (*a*) to purge his court of the bad; (*b*) to choose the good and able. Ch. IX: 1. How to judge of the ability of Ministers. 2. Distinction between wisdom and cunning. Ch. X: 1. That a patriot King ought to espouse no party. 2. The evil of governing by one, either in a State united or divided. Ch. XI: 1. How to conduct himself with regard to parties (*a*) even in the greatest extremities and? after a contrary conduct in former reigns. 2. A digression, applying this to the case of the Jacobites. Ch. XII: 1. Objections raised to the practicability of governing without a party, answered. 2. The original and causes of faction. 3. The example of Queen Elizabeth, as to party. Ch. XIII: 1. That, notwithstanding all objections, a King may be an honest man, and great, by patriotism. 2. That his interest and his country's will. be the same. 3. What is the particular and true interest of Great Britain?

With these may be compared the subjects taken up in *The Prince*: Ch. I. The various kinds of government and the ways by which they are established; Ch. II. Of hereditary monarchies; Ch. III. Of mixed monarchies; Ch. IV. Why the kingdom of Darius, occupied by Alexander, did not rebel against the successors of the latter after his death; Ch. V. The way to govern cities or dominions that, previous to being occupied, lived under their own laws; Ch. VI. Of new dominions which have been acquired by one's own arms and ability; Ch. VII. Of new dominions acquired by the power of others or by fortune; Ch. VIII. Of those who have attained the position of prince by villainy; Ch. IX. Of the civic principality; Ch. X. How the strength of all States should be measured; Ch. XI. Of ecclesiastical principalities; Ch. XII. The different kinds of militia and mercenary soldiers; Ch. XIII. Of auxiliary, mixed, and native troops; Ch. XIV. The duties of a prince with regard to the militia; Ch. XV. Of the things for which men, and especially princes, are praised or blamed; Ch. XVI. Of liberality and niggardliness; Ch. XVII. Of cruelty and clemency, and whether it is better to be loved or feared; Ch. XVIII. In what way princes must keep faith; Ch. XIX. That we must avoid being despised and hated; Ch. XX. Whether fortresses and other things which

of himself as continuing the form of the manual *de regimine principum*, but departing from its customary ethical attitudes at crucial points, while Bolingbroke meant to adhere to the ethical content of the tradition as well as to the form of the manual.

Bolingbroke's intention, derived from his cultural sympathies, is implicit in his title. Machiavelli had claimed to be describing a real prince as distinguished from the imaginary ones described by his predecessors. Bolingbroke, however, intends to describe for us the *idea* of a king. He will show how this idea may be embodied in the actual, as in the case of Queen Elizabeth, but his title makes it clear that he is primarily interested in deducing what a king should be according to reason, rather than in reflecting upon what kings have been. The Platonic connotation of the word 'idea' is significant, for it affiliates Bolingbroke with the cultural tradition which, by way of Shaftesbury, Glanville, and the Cambridge Platonists, leads back to Colet, More, and Erasmus, and thence to the Platonic humanists of the Florentine Academy, to Pico and Ficino. The first of the three large sections into which the argument of *The Idea of a Patriot King* is divided attempts to demonstrate, in accordance with the title, the rational 'idea' of a king, and the rational basis of limited monarchy. When Bolingbroke has set forth these general principles to his own satisfaction he turns to Machiavelli; the central portion of the book, which we will consider in Chapter VI, joins issue with Machiavelli over the problem of how to regenerate a corrupt state. The concluding portion of *The Idea of a Patriot King*, to be discussed in Chapter VII, concerns itself with the application of Bolingbroke's principles to England and to English history.

The word 'idea' in Bolingbroke's title, however, provides a clue to the ultimate nature of his opposition to Machiavelli. Experience in particular instances, Bolingbroke saw, did not always conform to rational patterns. Nevertheless, he thought, if one had enough experience, and chiefly if one knew enough history, the great regularities in experience would become

---

princes often contrive are useful or injurious; Ch. XXI. How a prince must act in order to gain reputation; Ch. XXII. Of the secretaries of princes; Ch. XXIII. How flatterers must be shunned; Ch. XXIV. Why the princes of Italy have lost their States; Ch. XXV. How much fortune can do in human affairs and how it may be opposed; Ch. XXVI. Exhortation to liberate Italy from the barbarians.

evident. The rational structure of thought might be seen to conform ultimately to the rational Nature of Things. What Bolingbroke felt he had found in history, and attempts to show by the examples he chooses, is confirmation of the classical tradition of natural law. He found, or believed he had found, confirmation of the proposition that virtuous behaviour, as traditionally understood, is based on principles which are not *simply* products of the ethical imagination, but which may also be seen to be inherent in the phenomenal world. He believed that the contravention of these principles brings, in the long run, inevitable disaster. This, in the final analysis, is the basis for his attack on Machiavelli.

Bolingbroke's original title, *The Patriot Prince*, had called attention more emphatically to his opposition to Machiavelli, by suggesting that Bolingbroke was going to set forth a conception of the prince which would stand in contrast to Machiavelli's.[8] It may be that he changed 'Prince' to 'King' in order to flatter Frederick by alluding to his prospects; or perhaps, considering Machiavelli's bad reputation, he thought better of claiming in his title too explicit a relationship to him. To have done so would have been to provide an obvious opening for the insinuations of his political enemies. Whatever the truth of this matter, however, it is clear that Bolingbroke was both attracted by Machiavelli and repelled by him. He felt the claims of the *realpolitik* solution (and perhaps here we may find a source for his admiration for Tacitus, who was, during the Renaissance, considered a Machiavellian), but he was repelled by its ultimate implications.

II

Bolingbroke's manual begins with an Introduction of about two thousand words, in which he touches upon some of the principal themes of the work itself. Before proceeding to the text of the manual proper, therefore, it will be worth while to consider some of the important points that come up in the Introduction.

Bolingbroke addresses the book to Lord Cornbury. There can be no doubt, however, in view of the political situation in

---

[8] Herbert Butterfield, *The Statecraft of Machiavelli* (London, 1955), p. 153.

England and Bolingbroke's role in it, that his readers were aware that the manual was, in fact, written for Prince Frederick. It may be that Bolingbroke adopted this strategy, allowing Frederick to listen, as it were, to a correspondence between two aristocrats, because he wished to emphasise the role of the ruling class in the structure of the government. Important as the king still was to the system, Bolingbroke would not have been inclined to suggest, as previous writers in this genre had done, that he alone was important. Bolingbroke's audience knew very well, however, that the book was written for Frederick, and in this respect Bolingbroke followed the pattern which had long been established for the genre. Machiavelli had addressed his to Lorenzo. Erasmus had addressed Charles; Petrus Bizzarus, Elizabeth; and Petrarch, in his *De republica optime administrando*, had similarly praised Francisco Carrara. Clichtoveus and Budé had likewise presented their manuals as gifts to monarchs. In so doing, it has been said, all these writers were following the example of Isocrates, in his address to Nicoles, which was one of the sources of the genre. Both Machiavelli and Bolingbroke, however, depart from the tradition by assuming that the ruler is in need of their advice. Their predecessors had been more humble. As Petrus Bizzarus had written at the beginning of his *De optimo principe*: 'For you (Most Serene Queen) exhortation of this sort is superfluous, since you never neglect anything which you think pertains to a true and legitimate rule, so that you are rather for other kings and princes a kind of form and idea (if I may so express it) of ruling well than in need of the precepts and encouragement of others.'[9] Both Machiavelli and Bolingbroke, perhaps imitating him here, are more assertive of their own qualifications for giving advice. Machiavelli tells Lorenzo, quite brazenly considering the tone usually employed in the addresses of such works, that he has acquired knowledge of the deeds of great men 'through a long experience of modern events and a constant study of the past', and that only a man

---

[9] '*Tibi vero (Serenissima Regina) supervacanea est huiusmodi exhortatio, cum nihil unquam praetermittas quod ad veram ac legitimam gubernationem pertinere animadvertas, adeo ut potius caeteris Regibus ac Principibus bene regendi quaedam (ut ita dixerim) forma ideaque sis, quam ut aliorum praeceptis et cohortatione indigeas.*' Petrarch had given such praise to Francesco Carrara in *De republicae optime administranda*, and Erasmus wrote to Charles in his dedication to the *Institutio*, '*Tuae Celsitudini nihil opus esse cujusquam monitis.*' (Your eminence does not need the admonitions of anyone.)

such as he can truly know the nature of princes. Machiavelli barely bothers to put it diplomatically: 'for in the same way that landscape painters station themselves in the valleys in order to draw mountains or high ground, and ascend an eminence in order to get a good view of the plains, so it is necessary to be a prince in order to know thoroughly the nature of the people, and one of the populace to know the nature of princes'.[10] Lorenzo, therefore, needs Machiavelli's instruction with respect to the subject-matter of this book, the nature of princes. He needs it, Machiavelli implies, because traditional writing on the subject has been misleading, has described things as they ought to be and not as they are. Writing as a member of 'the populace', Machiavelli can puncture illusion, and can show in what respects the traditional aristocratic-humanistic writers have been in error. Bolingbroke's similar arrogance proceeds from the opposite assumption. Whereas for Machiavelli princes were likely to have been misled by traditional morality, in Bolingbroke's view they are likely to have been misled by Machiavellianism. Bolingbroke writes as one detached from politics, takes the high tone of a man who has nothing to lose, and tries to restore the prince whom he is instructing to the old and genuine principles of statecraft. He writes, he says, as one stripped of his rights, but as a Briton still. 'I am not one of those oriental slaves, who deem it unlawful presumption to look their kings in the face. . . .' Possessing an intellectual arrogance equal to Machiavelli's, Bolingbroke prepares to defend tradition against him.

In the opening paragraphs of the book, referring to the *Letter on the Spirit of Patriotism*, Bolingbroke observes that he has already dealt with 'the duties which men owe to their country' —has considered, that is, the duties of the ruling class—and will now 'carry these considerations further, and . . . delineate, for I pretend not to make a perfect draught, the duties of a king to his country'.[11] He will set forth, he says, the duties which in principle a king owes to his country, and then apply such general principles to 'the present state of Great Britain'. Bolingbroke makes a considerable point of disclaiming belief in the divine right of kings: 'I know of none who are anointed

10 *The Prince*, Dedication.
11 *Bolingbroke*, II, p. 372.

by God to rule in limited monarchies.'[12] Nevertheless, when he comes later on to discuss the foundations of constitutional monarchy he comes very close to arguing that this system is in harmony with the rational nature of things and therefore sanctioned, in a sense, divinely. Of course, such a position would make the office of the king, and not his person, divinely sanctioned. In his politics as in his theology, Bolingbroke's conception of providence was general.

In addition to disclaiming belief in the doctrine of the divine right of monarchy, he also denies that there should be anything arcane or sacrosanct about the monarch. He will look kings in the face, he says, for 'no secrets are more important to be known, no hearts deserve to be pryed into with more curiosity and attention, than those of princes'.[13] The last word, 'princes', may be a reflection of his earlier title. At any rate, he proposes to do here just what Machiavelli had done; he will look in an analytic and detached way at princes. Though Machiavelli's perspective was that of 'one of the populace', and Bolingbroke writes as an exile stripped of hope and as an olympian student of the history of the ages, the studies will be equally free from illusion. Thus he makes a claim of objectivity resembling Machiavelli's, even while implying, in his title, that he will emerge with different prescriptions. And yet, though he was attempting to put the powers of the monarch on a firm basis, to shore them up, as it were, against the pressure of the oligarchy, the very objectivity which Bolingbroke feels required to assert may, ironically, have done much to subvert the position of the king, and indeed of the principle of authority in general. As Walter Lippmann has observed, the authority of government since the eighteenth century has been 'stripped . . . of that imponderable authority which is derived from tradition, immemorial usage, consecration, veneration, prescription, prestige, heredity, hierarchy' by 'the white light of the enlightenment and the secularisation of men's minds'.[14] Part of the drama of Bolingbroke's book is his effort to defend, in the language of the enlightenment, the traditionally recognised claims of government.

[12] Ibid.
[13] Ibid.
[14] Lippmann, *The Public Philosophy*, p. 56.

He not only claims analytical detachment, but also, in standard oratorical fashion, argues that no political self-interest motivates his reflections. He claims to be an impartial critic whom one can trust: 'But many things have concurred, besides age and temper, to set me at a great distance from the present court. Far from prying into the hearts, I scarce know the faces of our royal family.'[15] Of course, there is no doubt that it was not age and temper that removed him from power. Rather, he was forced out. Still, we must not be too quick to take such statements as evidence of insincerity. In writing a book such as this, Bolingbroke was not speaking simply in his own voice. He was writing in a well-known mode, and in so doing striking an attitude exemplary for advisers to princes. The 'I' that appears in his personal references is an artistic creation, derived from reality but not equal to it, much as the Milton of the prologues in *Paradise Lost* is an idealised version of the real Milton, and the Alexander Pope of the Horatian imitations, whether the plain honest man or the lofty poet of indignant scorn, is a *persona* only obliquely related to the real poet. The use of such *personae* was part of the technique of persuasion in the classical oration: if the writer can project so attractive an ideal of self, the implication is, his ideals in other respects will be equally valid.[16]

In the fourth paragraph of this Introduction, Bolingbroke reaffirms, in characteristic fashion, the principles of the laws of nature, as he calls them, which govern his political thought. They are the same, he says, as those that informed the *Letter on the Spirit of Patriotism*: 'The principles I have reasoned upon in my letter to my Lord——, and those I shall reason upon here, are the same. They are laid in the same system of human nature. They are drawn from that source from whence all the duties of public and private morality must be derived, or they will be often falsely, and always precariously, established. Up to this source there are few men who take the pains to go: and, open as it lies, there are not many who can find their way to it.'[17] Bolingbroke thus supposes, and in this he is supported

---

[15] *Bolingbroke*, II, p. 372.
[16] Aristotle, *Rhetoric*, I, 2.
[17] *Bolingbroke*, II, p. 373.

by many recent writers, that free institutions not grounded on such principles lead a precarious existence.[18]

In concluding this fourth paragraph of the Introduction, Bolingbroke expresses an opinion of the present condition of England which is rather gloomier than that set forth in the *Letter on the Spirit of Patriotism*, composed during the previous year. He had then hoped for much from the coming generation of political leaders: 'I expect little', he had then said, 'from the principal actors that tread the stage at present. . . . I turn my eyes from the generation that is going off, to the generation that is coming on the stage.' But in *The Idea of a Patriot King* he sees little hope in the coming generation: the greatest part of the present generation is corrupt, he says; they 'measure their interest by their passions, and their duty by the examples of a corrupt age'. Such, therefore, 'we may justly apprehend that the next will be; since they who are to compose it will set out into the world under a direction that must incline them strongly to the same course of self-interest, profligacy, and corruption'.[19]

Such deepened pessimism may reflect Bolingbroke's disappointment over the failure of the Opposition to make headway against Walpole during the preceding year, but whether or not this deeper pessimism has its source in current politics, it does define the starting-point for *The Idea of a Patriot King* considered as an exercise in political science. Assuming that England has become corrupt, by which he means that the vast majority of men, and particularly the nation's leaders, lack public spirit and are governed by mean motives, Bolingbroke addresses himself to the problem of corruption and its cure as set forth by Machiavelli in the middle chapters of the First Book of *The Discourses*. *The Idea of a Patriot King* thus proceeds on two levels which Bolingbroke sees as related. He is able to shift from polemic against Walpole to discussion of the classic problem dealt with by Machiavelli. 'Corruption' can thus mean a variety of things, from ordinary bribery to the degeneration that overtakes all states as they depart from their original principles. This pro-

---

[18] This is the argument of Lippmann's *The Public Philosophy* (Boston, 1955), of Ernest Barker's *Traditions of Civility* (Cambridge, 1948), of Peter Stanlis's *Burke and the Natural Law* (Ann Arbor, 1958), of Peter Viereck's *Conservatism Revisited* (London, 1950).

[19] *Bolingbroke*, II, p. 373.

cedure was aided by the rather striking appositeness of *The Discourses* to the situation in England as interpreted by Bolingbroke. So careful a student of Machiavelli as Bolingbroke could not but have been struck, for example, in the reign of George II, by the heading of Chapter XIX of the First Book: 'If an Able and Vigorous Prince is Succeeded by a Feeble One, the Latter May For a Time Be Able To Maintain Himself; But if His Successor Be Also Weak, Then the Latter Will Not Be Able to Preserve His State.'

In the next paragraph, the fifth of the Introduction, Bolingbroke combines a Burkean sense of the continuity of states with an indictment of Walpole. The effects of a bad administration, he says, are more serious than the actual crimes committed or their immediate consequences. Bad rulers 'sin against posterity as well as against their own age; and when the consequences of their crimes are over, the consequences of their example remain. I think, and every wise and honest man in generations yet unborn will think, if the history of this administration descends to blacken our annals, that the greatest iniquity of the minister, on whom the whole iniquity ought to be charged, since he has been so long in possession of the whole power, is the constant endeavour he has employed to corrupt the morals of men.'[20] So entrenched, by this time, have bad habits thus become that they will be very difficult to reform: a 'wiser and honester administration may draw us back to our former credit and influence abroad', may improve trade and pay off the debt, but 'will the minds of men, which this minister has narrowed to personal regards alone, will their views, which he has confined to the present moment, as if nations were mortal like the men who compose them, and Britain was to perish with her degenerate children; will these, I say, be so easily or so soon enlarged?'[21] In this paragraph Bolingbroke anticipates two of Burke's principal theses. In his emphasis upon the difficulty of correction under such circumstances he argues, as does Burke, that habit, as it were unconscious and resistant to the discipline of reason, is a primary force in political life. The schemes of sophistic reasoners, Burke would argue, could never comprehend the complex operations of long-developed habit. Boling-

[20] Ibid.
[21] Ibid., p. 374.

broke also anticipates Burke's conception of the State as a continuing entity. It is an error to suppose that Britain will perish with her degenerate children, i.e. that 'Britain' is equivalent to the generation now in power. Society, to achieve the purposes for which it exists—that is, for it to be able to civilise men, to foster the full development of human potentialities in philosophy, in art, in the cultivation of the spiritual life—must continue to exist for many generations. Society, therefore, in the view of Bolingbroke as of Burke, is more properly to be compared to a corporation than to an individual, for it lives on while individuals come into it and go out of it. Nations are not mortal like men, says Bolingbroke, and Britain will not perish with her degenerate children.

Society, said Burke, is a partnership, 'a partnership in all science; a partnership in all art; a partnership in every virtue, and in all perfection. As the ends of such a partnership cannot be obtained in many generations, it becomes a partnership not only between those who are living, but between those who are living, those who are dead, and those who are about to be born.' The importance of such a view, which transcends the short-range objectives of individual interests, is that it gives, as Walter Lippmann has well said, 'rational meaning to the necessary objectives of government':

> If we deny it, identifying the people with the prevailing pluralities who vote in order to serve, as Bentham puts it, 'their pleasures and their security', where and what is the nation, and whose duty is it to defend the public interest? Bentham leaves us with the state as an arena in which factions contend for their immediate advantage in the struggle for survival and domination. Without the invisible and transcendent community to bind them, why should they care for posterity? And why should posterity care about them, and about their treaties and their contracts, their commitments and their promises? Yet without these engagements to the future, they could not live and work; without these engagements the fabric of society is unravelled and shredded. [22]

The entire discussion of duty in Bolingbroke, as something which transcends individual interest, whether in his urging the duties

[22] Lippmann, *The Public Philosophy*, p. 36.

of public service upon the governing class in the *Letter on the Spirit of Patriotism*, or insisting that limitation of personal power is rational in *The Idea of a Patriot King*, should be seen as an attempt to provide principles upon which the community can continue to exist and so perform its proper tasks. Bolingbroke was concerned, as was Burke, to establish such principle in opposition to attitudes based upon a presumption that immediate self-interest ought to govern behaviour. Bolingbroke's opinion that self-aggrandisement must be limited by rational consideration of the claims of community is analogous to his sense, with respect to the life of the community, of the limitations of individual experience. It is very difficult, he argues in *On the Study and Use of History*, for one to achieve a sense of the entirety of an event, and individual experience, limited as it is in time, provides a poor basis for decision: 'Experience is doubly defective; we are born too late to see the beginning, and we die too soon to see the end of many things.' Just as self-interest must be limited by the claims of the community, so individual experience must be corrected by the knowledge of larger continuities.

In the paragraph under discussion, one notices, Bolingbroke declares that the objectives of the Opposition, even if achieved, will not in themselves be enough to regenerate England. The improvement of trade, relief from debt, the recovery of influence abroad—all planks in the Opposition platform—will not be enough if *habits* are not changed. Bolingbroke thus continues the moral emphasis which in the Humanist programme, as distinguished from that of Machiavelli, was so important. He 'who abandons or betrays his country', declares Bolingbroke, 'will abandon or betray his friend'.[23]

Bolingbroke concludes this fifth paragraph with a striking simile, reminiscent of Donne, which expresses his sense of the difficulty of reform:

> the progress from confirmed habits of evil is much more slow than the progress to them. Virtue is not placed on a rugged mountain of difficult and dangerous access, as they who would excuse the indolence of their temper, or the perverseness of their will, desire to have it believed; but she is seated, however, on an eminence. We may go up to her with ease, but we must go up gradually, according to the natural pro-

[23] *Bolingbroke*, II, p. 373.

gression of reason, who is to lead the way and guide our steps. On the other hand, if we fall from thence, we are sure to be hurried down the hill with a blind impetuosity, according to the natural violence of those appetites and passions that caused our fall at first, and urged it on the faster, the further they are removed from the control that before restrained them.[24]

Reason here is natural, and as such works slowly. But the passions, also natural, seem more powerful in Bolingbroke's account. They work *with* the slope, and they urge the 'fall' on faster 'the further they are removed from the control that before restrained them'. This highly qualified conception of the efficacy of reason—and it has analogues, as we will see, in Swift—is further evidence, if any is needed, that Bolingbroke was not in any sense a naïve optimist. Indeed, Bolingbroke emphasises the *difficulty* of reform: to recover public spirit, he says, 'much time is required; and a work which requires so much time, may, too probably, be never completed'.[25] When he considers the situation in England he admits, pessimistically, that it is 'more to be wished than hoped, that the contagion should spread no further than that leprous race, who carry on their skins, exposed to public sight, the scabs and blotches of their distemper'.[26]

But given the situation—and Bolingbroke assumes it to be as bad as possible—that the State has become thoroughly corrupt, how indeed can it be regenerated? This is the theoretical problem at the centre of the book. The following paragraph is short, and because it states the issue so clearly it should be quoted in full.

It seems to me, upon the whole matter, that to save or redeem a nation, under such circumstances, from perdition, nothing less is necessary than some great, some extraordinary conjuncture of ill fortune, or of good, which may purge, yet so as by fire. Distress from abroad, bankruptcy at home, and other circumstances of like nature and tendency, may beget universal confusion. Out of confusion order may arise; but it may be the order of a wicked tyranny, instead of the order of a just

[24] Ibid., p. 374.
[25] Ibid.
[26] Ibid.

monarchy. Either may happen: and such an alternative at the disposal of fortune is enough to make a State tremble! We may be saved, indeed, by means of a very different kind; but these means will not offer themselves, this way of salvation will not be opened to us, without the concurrence, and the influence, of a Patriot King, the most uncommon of all phenomena in the physical or moral world.

Nothing can so surely and so effectually restore the virtue and public spirit essential to the preservation of liberty and national prosperity, as the reign of such a prince.[27]

A corrupt State thus may, after catastrophic dissolution, be ordered by chance. Or else, it can be saved by a Patriot King.

The first thing one notices about Bolingbroke's conception of the problem is the religious vocabulary he employs in his statement of it. A nation 'falls' from virtue: 'On the other hand, if we fall from thence, we are sure to be hurried down the hill with a blind impetuosity. . . .' Once it has fallen, it exists in a state of sin: 'It is more to be wished than to be hoped, that the contagion should spread no further than that leprous race, who carry on their skins, exposed to public sight, the scabs and blotches of their distemper.' From this fallen state the nation can be rescued only by a saviour who is 'the most uncommon of all phenomena in the physical or moral world', elsewhere described as 'a standing miracle'. This saviour, moreover, redeems the corrupt State, as we will see, through a voluntary act of self-sacrifice: he limits his own desires, and provides a paradigm for a similar limitation on the part of the rest of the citizens. Until such salvation appears, Bolingbroke says, the nation can only try to deserve it, hold itself in a quasi-religious condition of *waiting*: 'If the blessing be withheld from us, let us deserve, at least, that it should be granted to us. If heaven, in mercy, bestows it on us, let us prepare to receive it, to improve it, and to co-operate with it.'[28] Bolingbroke's conception of the problem and its hypothetical solution thus corroborates Carl Becker's thesis that the eighteenth-century philosophers projected the traditional Christian experience in secular terms, that, in other words, they concretised the spiritual. Though Bolingbroke did not go so far as some of the radical philosophes and

[27] Ibid.
[28] Ibid., p. 375.

envision the goal of history as a state of bliss, he did participate in the secularisation of the spirit.

In his Introduction, Bolingbroke has now stated the problem, defined it in its larger theoretical bearings and also with respect to England. He has alluded to his own principles, though he has not elaborated upon them, and he has suggested the nature of his opponents' principles: in England, those of Walpole; in ethical thought, those of Machiavelli. He agrees with Machiavelli, moreover, that under the extreme conditions assumed as the starting-point of the discussion, only an extraordinary man can save the State, and he implies that such a man must be, not Machiavelli's Prince, but a Patriot King. Bolingbroke concludes the Introduction by presenting, in characteristic oratorical fashion, an idealised portrait of himself. It functions, as we have seen, as one of the techniques of persuasion:

> I speak as if I could take my share in these glorious efforts. Neither shall I recall my words. Stripped of the rights of a British subject, of all except the meanest of them, that of inheriting, I remember that I am a Briton still. I apply to myself what I have read in Seneca; *'officia, si civis amiserit, hominis exerceat'*. I have renounced the world, not in show, but in reality, and more by my way of thinking, than by my way of living, as retired as that may seem. But I have not renounced my country, nor my friends. . . . In that retreat, wherein the remainder of my days shall be spent, I may be of some use to them; since even from thence, I may advise, exhort, and warn them.

III

The opening paragraph of the text proper of *The Idea of a Patriot King* shows very clearly Bolingbroke's attitude toward the use of history. He says that one could find in history examples to illustrate and confirm constant and universal principles of human nature. The individual fact was not as important as the principles it illustrated or brought to light. 'We ought always to keep in mind', he urges in *On the Study and Use of History*, 'that history is philosophy teaching by examples how to conduct ourselves in all the situations of private and public life; that therefore we must apply ourselves to it in a philosophical spirit and manner; that we must rise from particular to general knowledge, and that we must fit ourselves for the society and business of mankind by accustoming our minds to reflect and meditate on the characters we find described, and the course of events we find related there.'[29] In history one may find 'certain general principles, and rules of life and conduct, which always must be true, because they are conformable to the invariable nature of things'.[30] But they may be found only if one approaches history 'as he would study philosophy'—by which Bolingbroke means moving, in so far as possible, to more and more general statements. One must do this, he says, because it is the general proposition which should guide one, the particular case providing only limited guidance because it is always in some degree unique.

> Particular examples may be of use sometimes in particular cases; but the application of them is dangerous. It must be done with the utmost circumspection, or it will be seldom done with success.[31]

Indeed, one of the secondary criticisms which Bolingbroke makes of Machiavelli is that he is too much inclined to dogmatise on the basis of a limited number of examples.

> I know not whether Machiavel himself is quite free from defect on this account: he seems to carry the use and application of particular examples sometimes too far. Marius and Catulus passed the Alps, met, and defeated the Cimbri beyond the frontiers of Italy. Is it safe to conclude from hence, that whenever one people is invaded by another, the invaded ought to meet and fight the invader at a distance from their frontiers? Machiavel's countryman, Guicciardin, was aware of the danger that might arise from such an application of examples.[32]

Instead of using particular examples to guide us in action, we should, as in the literary imitation of classical models, 'catch the spirit, if we can, and conform ourselves to the reason of them'.[33] Bolingbroke was too much aware of the processes of history to be as confident as Machiavelli had been in drawing

[29] Ibid., p. 191.
[30] Ibid., p. 193.
[31] Ibid., p. 192.
[32] Ibid.
[33] Ibid., p. 193.

conclusions from particular cases. He thus is aware of a tension between the uniqueness of the fact and those characteristics which it has in common with other facts, and which permit one to rise to 'general principles'. Recent political philosophers, indeed, have inclined toward Bolingbroke's solution of this problem. 'Historical analogies', according to Paul H. Nitze, 'have great utility in illuminating complex situations and in helping one to sort out the significant from the merely striking. But action based too closely on historical analogies is apt to be sterile and unimaginative.'[34]

Because he is concerned chiefly with the general truths to be found in history, Bolingbroke is impatient with those who go to history only as researchers or antiquarians. The mere researcher, Bolingbroke says, grows neither wiser nor better himself, and so, though his work may be useful to others, the researcher remains a kind of instrument. As for the antiquarians, they have produced little that is useful, Bolingbroke thinks, because the facts about antiquity are few and comparatively uncertain, and therefore difficult to generalise convincingly.[35]

In discussing the duties of kings, therefore, Bolingbroke says in the opening paragraph of *The Idea of a Patriot King* that he will not attempt to investigate the origins of monarchy in the distant past. He will not discover the duties of kings 'by any nice inquiry into the original of their institution'. Too little is certainly known, he argues, about the beginnings of government, and what facts we do have are relevant only to 'a few nations', scarcely adequate, that is, for the deduction of universal principles. He had demonstrated this to his own satisfaction in the third letter of *On the Study and Use of History*. After a lengthy consideration of both classical authors and the Old Testament—and his remarks on the Old Testament were considered scandalous by his contemporaries—he had concluded: 'We have therefore neither in profane nor in sacred authors such authentic, clear, distinct, and full accounts of the originals of ancient nations, and of the great events of those ages that are commonly called the first ages, as deserve to go by the name of history, or as afford sufficient materials for chronology and

[34] Paul H. Nitze, 'The Role of the Learned Man in Government', *Review of Politics*, XX (1958), p. 280.
[35] Bolingbroke.

history.'[36] Nevertheless, he maintains in *The Idea of a Patriot King* that though history cannot provide answers in this respect, men may find them 'in their own thoughts': 'I mean what this institution ought to have been, whenever it began, according to the rule of reason, founded in the common rights, and interests, of mankind.' Thus one might discover, through reflection, certain clear principles which history then, properly interpreted—'philosophically considered'—would confirm. One could determine what monarchy ought to have been, whatever research might turn up regarding what it *had* been.

The next two paragraphs explain why true principles, although traceable in one's own thoughts, appear to have been neglected so often. 'Private interest', Bolingbroke tells us, and 'superstition, two vices to which that staring timid creature man is excessively prone', have perplexed 'so plain a matter'.[37] Those who have been responsible for the perplexing turn out to be the familiar enemies of the humanist tradition: the Schoolmen, a self-seeking clergy, and the tyrannical rulers who use them and co-operate with them.

After establishing reflection as the primary way of discovering true principles, Bolingbroke turns, despite his caveat about the method, to an examination of the origins of monarchy 'in the early ages of those nations that are a little known to us'. Some men, he says, raised themselves to power by conquest, but others were raised to power by common consent because they were 'authors of such inventions, as were of general use to the well-being of mankind', and so 'were not only reverenced and obeyed during their lives, but worshipped after their deaths'.[38]

---

[36] *Bolingbroke*, II, 211. Cf. *On the Study and Use of History*, II, 175: 'A man must be as indifferent as I am to common censure or approbation, to avow a thorough contempt for the whole business of these learned lives; for all the researches into antiquity, for all the systems of chronology and history, that we owe to the immense labours of a Scalinger, a Bochart, a Petavius, an Usher, and even a Marsham. The same materials are common to them all; but these materials are few, and there is a moral impossibility that they should ever have more. They have combined these into every form that can be given to them; they have supposed, they have guessed, they have joined disjointed passages of different authors, and broken traditions of uncertain originals, of various people, and of centuries remote from one another as well as from ours. . . . In short, my lord, all these systems are so many enchanted castles; they appear to be something, they are nothing but appearances: like them, too, dissolve the charm, and they vanish from the sight.'

[37] *Bolingbroke*, II, p. 376.
[38] Ibid., p. 377.

This emphasis upon utility had been an important part of the humanist tradition from its beginnings. We think of Rabelais's passages on 'the herb Pantagruelion', or of his attacks on the lack of utility in scholastic education; of Raphael's advice to Adam in *Paradise Lost* that he concern himself with his own affairs rather than with cosmology; or of Swift's Brobding-nagians, whose studies are directed to what is useful in life.

Somewhat less important than such inventors, Bolingbroke tells us, were 'the founders of commonwealths, the lawgivers, and the heroes of particular states', who 'became gods of a second class'. Interestingly enough, Bolingbroke diverges some-what from Machiavelli at this point, in so far as he subordinates lawgivers and founders to inventors. This may reflect Boling-broke's more insistent universalism: a lawgiver benefits only one nation, but the great inventions are international in their effects.

New means of achieving pre-eminence, Bolingbroke says, soon unfortunately were devised. 'Merit had given rank; but rank was soon kept, and, which is more preposterous, obtained, too, without merit. Men were then made kings for reasons as little relevant to good government, as the neighing of the horse of the son of Hystaspes.'[39] Here confronting, as had Elyot and other Renaissance theoreticians, the problem of the relationship between rank and merit, Bolingbroke shows that he is well aware of the shortcomings of inherited power. 'Domitian, the worst, and Trajan, the best of princes, were promoted to the empire by the same title. Domitian was the son of Flavius, and the brother, though possibly the poisoner too, of Titus Ves-pasian: Trajan was the adopted son of Nerva.'[40] Inheritance did not, he makes it clear, guarantee ability or virtue; and indeed, he suggests, it might have been well 'to have made these royal people gods at once: as gods they would have done neither good nor hurt; but as emperors, in their way to divinity, they acted like devils'. A master of philosophe badinage, Bolingbroke even admires in passing the Chinese custom of having one's merit ennoble one's ancestors, rather than one's posterity.

[39] Ibid.
[40] Ibid.

Nevertheless, despite these reservations about hereditary monarchy, and despite the harsh things he has said about the doctrine of the divine right of kings, Bolingbroke concludes this opening section with the seemingly paradoxical declaration: 'I esteem monarchy above any other form of government, and hereditary monarchy above elective. I reverence kings, their office, their rights, their persons: and it will never be owing to the principles I am going to establish, because the character and government of a Patriot King can be established on no other, if their office and their right are not always held divine, and their persons always sacred.'[41] In the next section of his book he makes it clear why this declaration does not contradict what had gone before. The institution of monarchy, he attempts to demonstrate, is in harmony with reason and with the nature of man. Since this is the case, it must follow that the monarch rules, if he rules properly, in accord with the will of the 'Author of Nature'.

Bolingbroke begins by developing, in an important paragraph, the theory of the 'two laws'.

> Now, we are subject, by the constitution of human nature, and therefore by the will of the Author of this and every other nature, to two laws. One given immediately to all men by God, the same to all, and obligatory alike on all. The other given to man by man; and therefore not the same to all, or obligatory alike on all: founded indeed on the same principles, but varied by different applications of them to times, to characters, and to a number, which may be reckoned infinite, of other circumstances. By the first, I mean the universal law of reason; and by the second, the particular law, or constitution of laws, by which every distinct community has chosen to be governed.[42]

It will be seen that this is merely a restatement of the traditional conception of the analogy between the divinely contrived order of nature and the order of the State, familiar to Ulysses' speech in Act I of *Troilus and Cressida*, and given in much the same terms by Elyot, Spenser, Hooker, and Milton.[43] Through-

---

[41] Ibid., p. 378.
[42] Ibid., pp. 378-9.
[43] Cf. *The Government*, Book I, Ch. 1: *On Hymne of Heavenly Beautie*, ll, 22-133; *Laws of Eclesiastical Polity*, Book I, III, 2; *Paradise Lost*, V, ll, 468-505.

out this section, indeed, what Bolingbroke does is to modify the traditional language, but not the substance of the traditional position. He completes, indeed, the series of analogies common-place during the Renaissance—cosmic, political, and psychological—by making obedience to the law of nature and the law of the State synonymous with rationality.

> The obligation of submission to both, is discoverable by so clear and so simple an use of our intellectual faculties, that it may be said properly enough to be revealed to us by God: and though both these laws cannot be said properly to be given by him, yet our obligation to submit to the civil law is a principal paragraph in the natural law, which he has most manifestly given us. In truth we can no more doubt of the obligations of both these laws, than of the existence of the law-giver.[44]

Though God did not institute monarchy, Bolingbroke goes on to argue, nor any other particular form of government, the necessity of government as such can be deduced from the 'law of nature', i.e. from human nature. 'It follows, therefore, that he who breaks the laws of his country resists the ordinance of God, that is, the law of his nature.'

Such an argument, Bolingbroke makes it clear, does not sanction tyranny, for 'good government alone can be in the divine intention. God has made us to desire happiness; he has made our happiness dependent on society; and the happiness of society dependent on good or bad government. His intention, therefore, was that government should be good.'[45] Of course, it might immediately be asked, is there general agreement on what 'governing well' would mean? But this question occurs more readily to us than it would to Bolingbroke. His cultural tradition, which informs his conception of the rational and the natural, lies behind his conception of the just State. Among classical writers on the subject there was, as has been pointed out, something of a consensus that the best State in practice was one in which the Constitution, adopted by the consent of the people, was administered by gentlemen in accordance with the law. Since what the classical theorists admired had seemed

---

[44] *Bolingbroke*, II, p. 379.
[45] Ibid., p. 380.

for a long time suitable to England, a conception of what was 'natural' was near at hand for Bolingbroke. What his cultural tradition sanctioned was natural and rational; what it excluded was barbarous. Bolingbroke's scepticism, it is clear, was chiefly confined to questions of religious revelation. He was not in any sense a sceptic *culturally*.

He concludes this second section with a paragraph in which he distinguishes between the office of the king and the individual who occupies it. 'The office of the king is, then, of right divine, and their persons are to be reputed sacred. As men they have no such right, no such sacredness belonging to them: as kings, they have both, unless they forfeit them. Reverence for government obliges to reverence governors, who, for the sake of it, are raised above the level of other men. . . .' Bolingbroke's distance from Jacobinism, whose proponents indeed often used phraseology similar to his, is epitomised by his phrase 'reverence for government'.[46] He did not dream, as did the Jacobins, of a new Adam, transformed and redeemed by the revolution which emancipated him from restraint.[47]

In the third section this distance from Jacobinism is again made manifest. Bolingbroke justifies hereditary monarchy on practical grounds. He is at pains to point out that hereditary, as opposed to elective monarchy, is not intrinsically more 'sacred'. They are sacred alike, and this attribute is to be ascribed or not ascribed, to them, as they answer, or do not answer, the ends of their institution.[48] In dividing the kinds of government into hereditary monarchies and elective monarchies, and in discussing the merits of both, Bolingbroke followed not only Machiavelli, who divided governments into republics and principates, but other Renaissance theorists as well. For example, Franciscus Patricius Senensis (1412–94) had done the same. In the first chapter of his *De regno et regis institutione* he explains that it is not odd that he should compose that work after writing *De institutione reipublicae*, for many fundamental principles apply to both: 'It should therefore not be counted a fault in me if I have attempted both, since I am able to cite witnesses in earlier times and many others as well who have

[46] Ibid.
[47] Cf. Lippmann, *The Public Philosophy*, pp. 68–72.
[48] *Bolingbroke*, II, p. 380.

indulged in the same practice.'[49] Though he is defending
hereditary monarchy, Bolingbroke goes so far as to admit that
'Nothing can be more absurd, in pure speculation, than an
hereditary right in any mortal to govern other men.' Nevertheless, he goes on to say, 'in practice, nothing can be more absurd
than to have a king to choose at every vacancy of a throne'.[50]
He has two main arguments to make against elective monarchy
(the form which, in the opinion of some political scientists, is
used in the United States).[51] The multitude, he says, 'would do
at least as well to trust to chance as to choice, and to their
fortune as to their judgment'.[52] In addition, the very process of
election often causes trouble: 'in elective monarchies, these
elections, whether well or ill made, are often attended with such
national calamities, that even the best reigns cannot make
amends for them: whereas, in hereditary monarchy, whether a
good or a bad prince succeeds, these calamities are avoided'.
One can sense here Bolingbroke's personal experience of
eighteenth-century election procedures—the methods used to

[49] '*non igitur hoc mihi vitio dandum erit si utrunque tenatvero, quum possim superiores
testes et complures etiam alios citare qui identidem quoque factitarunt.*' Machiavelli had
pointed out in the second chapter of *The Prince* that 'the difficulty of maintaining
hereditary states accustomed to a reigning family is far less than in new monarchies;
for it is sufficient not to transgress ancestral usages, and to adapt oneself to unfore-
seen circumstances; in this way such a prince will be able to maintain his position,
unless some very excessive and exceptional force deprives him of it; and even if
he be thus deprived, on the slightest mischance happening to the new occupier,
he will be able to regain it'. Egidio had agreed: 'Habit is as it were another nature;
hence by custom various kinds of government are made as it were natural. Therefore if through daily habit the people has obeyed fathers, sons, and the sons of sons,
it is as though by nature inclined to voluntary obedience. Hence, since anything
voluntary is less onerous and difficult, if the people is to obey freely and easily the
commands of the king, it is expedient that successions to the kingly dignity should
be hereditary.' Patricius had argued in similar vein, 'the son reigns without peril
who treads exactly in the footsteps of the parent who preceded him'.
[50] *Bolingbroke*, II, 380. Bolingbroke elsewhere recognised the tension that may
obtain between custom and the critical judgment. As he said in *On the Study and
Use of History*, 'I do not affect singularity. On the contrary, I think that a due
deference is to be paid to received opinions, and that a due compliance with
received customs is to be held; though both the one and the other should be, what
they often are, absurd and ridiculous. But this servitude is outward only, and
abridges in no sort the liberty of private judgment. The obligations of submitting
to it likewise, even outwardly, extend no further than to those opinions and
customs which cannot be opposed, or from which we cannot deviate, without
doing hurt, or giving offence to society' (II, 173).
[51] Cf. Clinton Rossiter, *The American Presidency* (New York, 1960), pp. 81–82.
[52] *Bolingbroke*, II, p. 380.

win elections as well as the passions that attended them. He
sees, because he had had experience in government, that im-
perfection is the condition of society. Without elections there is

> one source of evil the less open: and one source of evil the less
> in human affairs, where there are so many, is sufficient to de-
> cide. We may lament the imperfections of our human state,
> which is such, that in cases of the utmost importance to the
> order and good government of society, and by consequence to
> the happiness of our kind, we are reduced, by the very consti-
> tution of our nature, to have no part to take that our reason can
> approve absolutely. . . . In truth, all that human prudence
> can do, is to furnish expedients, and to compound, as it were,
> with general vice and folly.[53]

In discussing this problem Bolingbroke was not original; indeed, he was following the pattern prescribed by his tradition.[54]
Circumstances, however, forced him to be original in some of
the emphases of his treatment. Though Machiavelli realised
that the real alternatives for Italy were hereditary monarchy
on the one hand and new, or usurped, monarchies on the other,
his real admiration was for republican Rome and its historian,
Livy. Republican Rome remains as an ideal for him, even
though he thinks, as does Bolingbroke, that a corrupt State can
be reformed only by one man. Bolingbroke, on the other hand,
shows little enthusiasm for republicanism, even in hypothesis.
His conclusion to *The Idea of a Patriot King* echoes the Fourth
Eclogue of Virgil, looks to a reconstructed Empire. His exem-
plars are first Elizabeth and then Augustus, and the cadences
of his prose emulate the characteristic mood of Virgil, the poet
of empire.

Bolingbroke decides, then, that a limited, hereditary
monarchy is best: 'as I think a limited monarchy the best of
governments, so I think an hereditary monarchy the best of

[53] Ibid., p. 381.

[54] Cf. Egidio Colonna, *De regimine* 3.2.5: '*Consuetudo est quasi altera natura:
propter quod regimina ex consuetudine efficiuntur quasi naturalia. Populus ergo si per diuturnam
consuetudinem obedivit patribus, filiis, et filiorum filiis, quasi naturaliter inclinantur ut
voluntario obediant; quare cum omne voluntarium sit minus onerosum et difficile, ut libentius
et facilius obediat populus mandatis regis, expedit regiae dignitati per hereditatem succedere*';
Patricius, *De regno et regis institutione*, Ch. 1, explains that since he has written about
republicanism he will now write about monarchy: '*non igitur hoc mihi vitio dandum
erit si utrunque tentavero, quum possim superiores testes et complures etiam alios citare qui
identidem quoque factitarunt*'.

monarchies'.[55] He argues for the superior stability of monarchy as the dominating principle of government. 'When monarchy is the essential form, it may be more easily and more usefully tempered with monarchy.' Though the attempt to alter aristocratic government or democratic government in the direction of monarchy will tend to disrupt them, 'very considerable aristocratical and democratical powers may be grafted on a monarchical stock without . . . alter[ing] in any degree the essential form'.[56] He agrees with Hobbes that sovereignty must be 'absolute, unlimited, and uncontrollable power lodged somewhere in every government . . .', but argues that this power need not reside exclusively in the monarch. He thus envisions a 'mixed government', in which the Crown shares power with other elements in the government, and he attributes to the entire government the sovereignty called for in the theory of Hobbes. This conception—that the best régime was one combining kingship, aristocracy, and democracy—was in accord with the most influential classical theory on the matter.[57] Recent considerations of eighteenth-century government, indeed, give reasons which tend to validate Bolingbroke's concern for the balancing of the various elements within the government.[58]

[55] *Bolingbroke*, II, p. 381.

[56] Ibid. Burke referred to this opinion with approval in *Reflections on the Revolution in France* (London, 1953), p. 122: 'He says, that he prefers a monarchy to other governments; because you can better ingraft any description of republic on a monarchy than anything of monarchy upon the republican forms. I think him perfectly in the right. The fact is so historically; and it agrees well with the speculation.'

[57] Leo Strauss, *Natural Right and History* (Chicago, 1957), p. 142.

[58] Betty Kemp, *King and Commons* 1660–1832 (London, 1957), p. 2: 'The fight between King and Commons in the seventeenth century restricted the King's powers without making the Commons his master, even in the financial sphere, and to contemporaries at least it was remarkable that the Commons remained so long content with an incomplete victory. Because they did, the relationship between King and Commons in the eighteenth century was, for the first and last time, a balanced relationship between two more or less equal partners, of which the second did not owe all its powers, nor indeed entirely its existence, to the first.

'Constitutional theory supported the relationship, for it taught that a balance between independent and strong powers prevented tyranny. And perhaps it did. For when the balance between King and Commons was at length undermined, the undermining was due, not to the growth in power of one at the expense of the other, but to the advent of a freer and more independent electorate, no longer seriously influenced by the King and not checked or balanced by any other power.'

In the next paragraph, a remarkable and significant one, Bolingbroke reverts to the traditional conception that an analogy exists between the government of the State and the government of the universe. God himself, Bolingbroke argues, is in a sense a limited monarch, for he submits to the limitations imposed on his will by the fitness of things. This affirmation that God's powers are limited is not a mere hyperbole, but is to be identified with one position in a controversy of long standing. The most notable exponents of the opposing positions had been Thomas Aquinas and Duns Scotus, with Aquinas maintaining that God's omnipotence was limited by his rationality, that he could not, because his essence was reason, will the irrational, while Duns Scotus refused to place this limitation upon God's omnipotence. God could, Scotus thought, will the irrational.[59] The choice between these alternatives may be seen

[59] 'Duns Scotus' desire to guarantee as completely as possible the originality of the individual is closely related to his conception of the pre-eminence of will and to his doctrine of liberty in man. For him, as for Saint Thomas, it is certainly the will that wills and the intelligence that knows, but the fact that the will can command acts of understanding seems to him to decide in favour of the primacy of will. . . . This affirmation of the primacy of nobility of the will over the intellect in man announces a more voluntarist than intellectualist conception of liberty and that is precisely what we find in Duns Scotus' doctrine. . . . Because he considers finite beings in the light of Infinite Being, the theologian knows that God is absolutely omnipotent; that he is free to create or not, and to act through secondary causes or not; that he is omnipresent to all creatures and free to set up any moral code he pleases so long as it deals with rules of human conduct whose relation to his own essence are not necessary ones. Nothing of what depends on the free decisions of this absolutely free God is philosophically deducible.' (Etienne Gilson, *History of Christian Philosophy in the Middle Ages* (New York, 1954), pp. 463-4. 'That there was a Law of Nature was not doubted, nor that it flowed from a source superior to the human lawgiver and so was absolutely binding upon him. Such was the case whatever solution might be found for that deep reaching question of scholastic controversy which asks whether the essence of Law is Will or Reason. . . . Aquinas and his followers . . . derived the content of the Law of Nature from the Reason that is immanent in the Being of God and is directly determined by that *Natura Rerum* which is comprised in God Himself. . . . Immediately from this he derives the Lex Laturalis which is grounded in the participation by Man, as a reasonable being, in the moral order of the world. . . . The opposite party taught that Law becomes Law merely through the Will that this or that shall pass for Law and be binding. . . . In the later philosophy of Law the derivation of all Law from Will and the explanation of both Natural and Positive Law as mere command was well-nigh universal. Only Leibniz (1646–1716), who in so many directions went deeper than his contemporaries, and who, perhaps for this reason, so often turned his eyes backwards towards medieval ways of thought, disputed this "Will-Theory" with powerful words directed against Pufendorf and Cocceji. He denied the essentialness of the

to have profound political and psychological implications. Man, made in God's image, will be, or at least will strive to be, according to the position he adopts in this dispute, a creature of reason or a creature of will. If he is a creature of reason, he will look for happiness in the principle of limitation. If he is a creature of will, however, two possibilities are available, both of which Bolingbroke would have rejected. First, he may, like such Romantics as Nietzsche, conceive the goal of life to be the manifestation of power. Or else, if he thinks of the will as corrupt, he will, like Calvin, depend entirely on God's power for redemption. The position espoused by Aquinas is consistent with Bolingbroke's conception that a monarch ought to limit his own power voluntarily even when, the State being corrupt, he has the opportunity to gain absolute power. He *desires* limitation because he is rational. The principle of limitation, it will be seen, is also consistent with a classicist aesthetic, which celebrates and embodies in a variety of characteristic forms the principle of limitation. The Scotist position, on the other hand, is consistent with arbitrary rule, with the power-oriented psychology of Machiavelli and Nietzsche, and with a Romantic aesthetics. When Pope attacks 'dunces'—i.e. the descendants of Duns Scotus—in the name of classical ethics and aesthetics, he has given his enemies, by implication, the proper philosophic filiation.

Bolingbroke's position in this decisive matter is the one most frequently encountered among manuals *de regimine principum*. Clichtoveus had entitled his fifth chapter 'That the Prince Should Be Subject to the Laws and By His Example and the Probity of His Life Influence His Subjects Toward Virtue'.[60] Aquinas wrote that—and the attitude he shows here is characteristic of him—a king should take his example from God and 'correct what is grown to excess'.[61] The traditional attitude saw

---

[60] '*Quod principem legibus subditum esse decet: et suo exemplo vitaeque probitate subditos ad virtutem inducere.*'

[61] See *De regimine principum*, 1.15: '*quid inordinatum est corrigere*'. According to Aquinas, 'it is the king's responsibility . . . by his laws and instructions, by rewards and punishments, to keep from iniquity the men subject to him, and

---

idea of Compulsion in the idea of Law, and argued that *Recht* was prior to *Gesetz.*' (Otto Gierke, *Political Theories of the Middle Ages*, trans. F. W. Maitland (Cambridge, 1958), note 256.)

only danger in excess, in the indulgence of will, and accordingly identified well-being with limitation.

Bolingbroke does not suppose that we can know the 'reason' which limits God's omnipotence: 'I would not say God governs by a rule that we know, or may know, as well as he, and upon our knowledge of which he appeals to men for the justice of his proceedings toward them; which a famous divine has impiously advanced, in a pretended demonstration of his being and attributes.'[62] According to Bolingbroke, God's natural attributes may be known *a posteriori*: 'When we contemplate the works of God . . . they give us very clear and determined ideas of wisdom and power, which we call infinite, because they pass, in the exercise of them, all the bounds of our conceptions.'[63] Bolingbroke does not, however, in spite of Warburton's opinion to the contrary, deny that we can have any knowledge at all of God's moral attributes. His position in this respect is implied in the phraseology quoted above from *The Idea of a Patriot King*: 'I would not say God governs by a rule that we know, or may know, as well as he. . . .' Bolingbroke, in contrast to such rational theologians as Clarke, is concerned to preserve the distance of man from God: 'by ascribing to God not human notions and passions, but something, whatever it be, equivalent to these, King might, though he does not, reason as dogmatically as Clarke, a priori, from what the creator and governor of the world ought to do in those qualities, to what he has done. . . .'[64] Bolingbroke objects to Clarke's conception because he thinks it blasphemous to assert that God's conception of justice is the same thing as man's, but he does not wish to go so far as to say that they are totally different things, for that

---

[62] *Bolingbroke*, II, 382. The divine here alluded to may be Samuel Clarke, whose *A Demonstration of Being and Attributes of God* Bolingbroke had attacked in his philosophical writings.

[63] Bolingbroke, *Works*, V (London, 1754), 309–10.

[64] Ibid., p. 541.

---

influence them toward virtuous deeds, taking his example from God, who gives law to men, and bestows a reward on those who observe them and penalties on those who transgress'. (*'Cura imminet regi . . . ut suis legibus et praeceptis, poenis et praemiis homines sibi subjectos ab iniquitate coerceat, et ad opera virtuosa inducat, exemplum a Deo accipiens, qui hominibus legem dedit, observantibus quidem mercedem, transgrentientibus poenas retribuens.'*)

would be to say that we do not know what we are talking about when we say that God is just. Bolingbroke tries to solve the problem by making God's moral attributes, his goodness and justice, a part of his natural attribute, wisdom. God's works show his wisdom, and since God is wise, 'he does always that which is fittest to be done. That, which is fittest to be done, is always just and good.'[65] Like Swift and Pope, Bolingbroke sees presumption, or pride, as man's chief fault. In his view, the rational theologians presume too much when they ascribe to God human notions of justice. He yet does not wish to go as far as Hume was to go and deny that any correspondence can be maintained between divine and human attributes. For Bolingbroke, the moral order which governs the universe is not entirely commensurate with man's ability to apprehend it, but some of the principal characteristics of it may nevertheless be known. 'God does always that which is fittest to be done', and the fitness 'results from the various natures, and more various relations of things: so that, as creator of all systems by which these natures and relations are constituted, he prescribed to himself the rule, which he follows as governor of every system of being. In short, with reverence be it spoken, God is a monarch, yet not an arbitrary but a limited monarch, limited by the rule which infinite wisdom prescribes to infinite power.'[66] This conception of a comprehensive but partially incomprehensible order is identical with that elaborated by Pope five years before in *An Essay on Man*: it is presumptuous to 'scan' God, but one can be certain of some of his characteristics by considering the fitness of things. It is a conception that forms the metaphysical anchor of Bolingbroke's political philosophy, and his opinion that the true king, the Patriot King, who rules by divine right in the sense that he rules as God does, desiring to obey the principle of limitation. The king thus not only obeys the law, but wills his own obedience: 'If governing without any rule, and by arbitrary will, be not essential to our idea of the monarchy of the Supreme Being, it is plainly ridiculous to

---

[65] Ibid., p. 313.
[66] *Bolingbroke*, II, 382. Cf. Walter Lippmann: 'The modern trouble (in governing) is in a low capacity to believe in precepts which restrict and restrain private interests and desires. Conviction of the need of these restraints is difficult to restore once it has been radically impaired' (p. 114).

suppose them necessarily included in the idea of a human monarchy.'[67]

Bolingbroke's attitude, in this respect as in others, has a venerable pedigree. Egidio, following Aristotle, had expounded the traditional distinction between the king and the tyrant,[68] and the distinction had been fundamental, from Aristotle through the schoolmen to Bracton and Fortescue, and to the Renaissance humanists, and thence to the Augustan humanists of the eighteenth century.[69] The belief in an objective moral order is at the centre of Bolingbroke's quarrel with Machiavelli. Machiavelli's prince corresponds to the tyrant as defined by Clichtoveus: 'the king lives in subjection to the laws, which he observes to the utmost, but the tyrant wishes to be subject to no laws; he wishes merely to give laws to others, but not to receive them. Still further, whatever pleases him has for him the power of law, for the tyrant is not guided by right reason and does not investigate what is just and unjust.'[70]

Bolingbroke does not intend that the limitations he proposes upon the power of the king will be such as to vitiate it. 'There are limitations indeed that would destroy the essential form of monarchy; or, in other words, a monarchical constitution may be change under pretence of limiting the monarch.'[71] This, he says, is what happened during the rebellion of the seventeenth

[67] *Bolingbroke*, II, p. 382.

[68] '*Tangit autem Philosophus V Politicorum quatuor differentias inter tyrannum et regum. Prima est, quia rex respicit bonum commune: tyrannus vero bonum proprium. Nam regnum est principatus rectus, tyrannis vero est dominum perversum. Cum ergo bonum gentis sit divinius bono unius, perverse dominatur qui spreto bono communi intendit bonum proprium. Ex hac autem differentia prima sequitur secunda, videlicet quod tyrannus intendit bonum delectabile: rex vero bonum honorificum.*' (In the Fifth Book of the *Politics* the Philosopher touches on four differences between the tyrant and the King. The first is that the King is concerned with the common good, the tyrant with his individual good. For monarchy is a proper form of government, but the rule of a tyrant is a perverse form. Since therefore the good of the people is more divine than the good of one man, he rules perversely who, despising the common good, looks out for his personal good. And from this first difference rises the second, namely, that the tyrant is intent on a good that brings pleasure, but the King on a good that is honourable.) (*De regimine*, 3.2.6.)

[69] John Bowle, *Western Political Thought* (New York, 1949), Ch. III, IV, V; also Ernest Barker, *The Politics of Aristotle* (Oxford, 1946), pp. xlvii–lxii.

[70] '*Quod rex vitam agit legibus subditus: quas ad unguem observat. Tyrannus vero nullis legibus esse vult subjectus: sed leges tantum aliis dare non accipere. Immo quicquid ei placuerit: id apud ipsum vim legis habet. Quoniam recta ratione non ducitur tyrannus: neque disquirit quid iustum sit vel quid iniquum.*' (*De regis officio*, 5, folio 20, recto.)

[71] *Bolingbroke*, II, p. 383.

century, 'when the vilest usurpation, and the most infamous tyranny, were established over our nation, by some of the worst and some of the meanest men in it'.[72] Rather, he concludes, his 'aim is to fix this principle; that limitations on a crown ought to be carried as far as it is necessary to secure the liberties of a people; and that all such limitations may subsist, without weakening or endangering monarchy'.[73] He claims that this position differs from those he ascribes to both the Tories and the Whigs: 'I think on these subjects, neither as the Tories, nor as the Whigs have thought; at least, I endeavour to avoid the excesses of both. I neither dress up kings like so many burlesque Jupiters, weighing the fortunes of mankind in the scales of fate, and darting thunderbolts at the heads of rebellious giants; nor do I strip them naked, as it were, and leave them at most a few tattered rags to clothe their majesty, but such as can serve really as little for use as for ornament.'[74] Thus, in his attitude toward monarchy, as in his position in the theological debate on God's attributes, Bolingbroke attempts to occupy a middle position. It is clear, too, that in the above quotation he is using the terms Tory and Whig normatively, rather than with reference to actual political parties. Yet it is possible to doubt that, at the time Bolingbroke was writing, very many of either the Tories or the Whigs would have disagreed with his words. Very few disciples of Filmer, and very few republicans, were influential in political affairs.

Bolingbroke next takes up the theoretical objections which might be made to his position. Perhaps the limitations appropriate to the government of a bad prince will only hamper a good one, deprive his subjects of benefits, 'clog his administration'. Bolingbroke argues that this would not be the case. 'Our constitution is brought, or almost brought, to such a point, a point of perfection I think it, that no king, who is not, in the true meaning of the word, a patriot, can govern Britain with ease, security, honour, dignity, or indeed with sufficient power and strength. But yet a king, who is a patriot may govern with all the former; and, besides them, with power as extended as the most absolute monarch can boast, and a power too, far

[72] Ibid.
[73] Ibid.
[74] Ibid.

more agreeable in the enjoyment as well as more effective in the operation.'[75] What Bolingbroke is saying here may best be understood in the light of Betty Kemp's analysis of the relations between King and Commons as they existed at the time Bolingbroke was writing. If, as she says, 'the relationship between King and Commons in the eighteenth century was, for the first and last time, a balanced relationship between two more or less equal partners',[76] then the monarch, to maintain his power *vis-à-vis* the Commons, and to play his part in such a balanced Constitution, must rule with broad support. He cannot be the representative of a faction, for that would diminish his power, make him, in the end, dependent on the faction. Nor, if he is to function with all his proper powers, can he rule for the sake of his own private aggrandisement. On the other hand, if he rules with widespread support—if he is, in Bolingbroke's sense of the word, a 'patriot'—then he will be able to perform his proper role in the government and, because of the power resulting from the harmonious working of the government, be in the end more powerful than the tyrant or the leader of a faction.

[75] Ibid.
[76] Kemp, *King and Commons* 1660–1832, p. 2.

VI

THE HEART OF THE
MACHIAVELLIAN PROBLEM

PERCEPTIVE readers during the 1740s would not have been surprised by Bolingbroke's attempt in *The Idea of a Patriot King* to combine an attack upon Walpole with an anti-Machiavel. In the *Fables* and in *The Beggar's Opera* Gay had linked Walpole with Machiavelli,[1] and Swift had made the same connection by innuendo in *Gulliver's Travels*.[2] In *Jonathan Wild*, which was published in 1743, Fielding constructed an attack upon Walpole which was at the same time an elaborate parody of Machiavelli.[3] These writers could count on an understanding of their intention at least among sophisticated readers, for Machiavelli was widely read in Nevile's translation and there had been considerable discussion of his work.[4] Where Boling-

---

[1] For the use of Machiavellian themes in *The Beggar's Opera* and the *Fables*, see Sven Armens, *John Gay: Social Critic* (New York, 1954), Ch. VII.

[2] Edwin Benjamin, 'The King of Brobdingnag and Secrets of State', JHI, XVIII (1957), 572–9, demonstrates the anti-Machiavellian character of many of the allusions in Book II, Ch. 7 of *Gulliver's Travels*. For example, the King of Brobdingnag professed to 'despise all mystery, refinement, and intrigue, either in a prince or a minister. He could not tell what I meant by secrets of state. . . .' The language here and elsewhere in the chapter would have suggested Machiavelli (mystery, refinement, and intrigue) and Walpole (*secrets of State* was one of Walpole's favourite defences against parliamentary enquiry). See also Jeffrey Hart, 'The Ideologue as Artist: Some Notes on *Gulliver's Travels*', *Criticism*, II (1960), 125–33, for an elaboration upon this theme.

[3] See Bernard Shea, 'Machiavelli and *Jonathan Wild*', PMLA, LXXII (1957), 55–73.

[4] Between 1675 and 1762 Nevile's translation of Machiavelli's *Works* was the only complete edition of his writings available in English. Fielding owned this edition, and quoted from it in the *Champion*. According to Bernard Shea, cited above, he used Nevile in writing *Jonathan Wild*. Pope had read Machiavelli, and

broke differs from such political allies of his as Gay, Swift, and Fielding, however, is in the explicitness of his relationship to Machiavelli. He does not make his point by hint and allusion, but attempts to launch a serious attack upon some of Machiavelli's most important theories. The other writers used Machiavelli as a conventional symbol for amoral politics, which they also associated with Walpole, but Bolingbroke set out to analyse the consequences of Machiavelli's approach to particular political problems.

In the preceding chapter we have seen how in the early parts of *The Idea of a Patriot King* Bolingbroke attempts to establish his general principles of statecraft. In the central section of the book he turns to a characteristically Machiavellian problem: how is the corrupt state to be regenerated? He agrees with the thesis set forth in *The Discourses* that the regeneration of the corrupt state must be the work of a single extraordinary man, but tries to argue in contradiction to Machiavelli that even in such an emergency success ultimately depends upon the maintenance of traditional moral values. Whether or not we judge Bolingbroke to be correct in his interpretation of Machiavelli, or in the solution he attempts for the problem Machiavelli poses, we see that he has learned from Machiavelli throughout, conceives of the problem in Machiavellian terms; and yet, though at times his argument even paraphrases Machiavelli, he breaks with Machiavelli at decisive points and argues for the superiority of the traditional moral position. By so doing he hopes to show that even when Machiavelli is encountered on the ground he had made peculiarly his own, that is, on the question of the extreme situation which appears to suspend

---

was of the opinion that Machiavelli generalised too widely from particulars and hence gave a false impression of the causes of human actions (see George Sherburn, 'Pope at Work', in *Essays on the Eighteenth Century Presented to David Nicol Smith* (Oxford, 1945), pp. 50–51). This was a criticism which many others had made, such as Guicciardini, Bolingbroke, and, in the twentieth century, Herbert Butterfield. In his *Dialogues of the Dead*, in a dialogue between Guise and Machiavelli, George Lyttelton put forward the theory that *The Prince*, which he took to be an exposition of the principles of absolutism, was an instance of vanity. Henry Nevile, the translator of Machiavelli, interpreted *The Prince* as a satire upon the abuses characteristic of tyranny. The majority of such commentators on Machiavelli seem to have respected Machiavelli as an historian and as a political analyst, but they found repellent his pessimistic view of human nature, which ran counter to the widespread hope of improving men through appeal to their moral sense.

generally accepted values, his solutions are faulty and traditional values applicable. Bolingbroke thus continues the anti-Machiavellian tradition which had been characteristic of English humanism. The point to be recognised about Bolingbroke's manual for the prince, accordingly, is not, as Plumb says, that it is full of commonplaces.[5] It *is*, of course. The important thing is that Bolingbroke intended his arguments to be recognised as a reassertion of the familiar, intended them to be polemical affirmations of the traditional position. Indeed, the significance of the book might be said to lie in the fact that so much of it is *not* original. Prior to *The Prince*, or in the work of a writer who had not read it, the traditional principles might fairly be characterised as commonplaces; that is, as uttered in ignorance of the pressure of alternatives. But in *The Idea of a Patriot King* the assertion of these principles is consciously aggressive, critical of what Bolingbroke understood Machiavelli's position to be.

As we have seen, Bolingbroke considered that England under the Hanoverians had become corrupt, and he intended in *The Idea of a Patriot King* to set forth a prescription for the corrupt state. Like Machiavelli, he held to the theory that states have a tendency to degenerate, to grow older and decay much as individuals do. In expressing this view in *The Idea of a Patriot King* he paraphrased a famous passage from *The Discourses*:

> The best instituted governments, like the best constituted animal bodies, carry in them the seeds of their destruction: and though they grow and improve for a time, they will soon tend visibly to their dissolution. Every hour they live is an hour the less that they have to live. All that can be done, therefore, to prolong the duration of a good government, is to draw it back, on every favourable occasion, to the first good principles on which it was founded. When these occasions happen often, and are well improved, such governments are prosperous and durable. When they happen seldom, or are ill improved, these political bodies live in pain, or in languor, and die soon.[6]

The degenerate state, in Bolingbroke's view as in Machiavelli's,

[5] J. H. Plumb, *The First Four Georges* (London, 1956), p. 79.
[6] *The Works of Lord Bolingbroke*, II (Philadelphia, 1841), p. 396. Cf. *The Discourses*, Book III, Ch. 1.

is one which, like Lilliput or Balnibarbi, has departed from earlier virtuous principles. A state must therefore be regularly refounded, returned to its earlier principles, if it is not to perish, and the maintenance of the state, like the maintenance of virtue quoted earlier from *The Idea of a Patriot King*, is a task which must be accomplished despite a pervasive degenerative tendency.

Machiavelli deals with the problem of regenerating the corrupt state in a variety of places, most importantly in Chapters IX, X, XVII, XVIII, and XIX of Book One of *The Discourses* and in the first chapter of Book Three. The problem is also, of course, the *raison d'être* of *The Prince*. The disorders of Italy, we are given to understand, though they are a special instance of corruption in that they are caused by foreign domination, can be cured, like other kinds of corruption, by the man of *virtu*, the man who effectively combines the qualities of the lion and the fox.

Since Bolingbroke's discussion of the methods of overcoming corruption in the State has as its basis Machiavelli's analysis in *The Prince* and *The Discourses*, it will be useful to review here, before considering Bolingbroke's prescription, what Machiavelli has to say on the subject. Discussing in Chapter IX of Book I the murder of Remus by Romulus, and the subsequent killing of Titus Tatius, Machiavelli observes that 'a wise mind will never censure anyone for having employed extraordinary means for the purpose of establishing a kingdom or constituting a republic', and that furthermore 'as a general rule . . . it never or rarely happens that a republic or monarchy is well constituted or its old institutions entirely reformed, unless it is done by only one individual'.[7] Violence on the part of such a founder as Romulus is justified, Machiavelli argues, since it was employed for good ends, for 'the general good and not for the gratification of his own ambition', and the freedom of Romulus from self-interest is proved, for Machiavelli, by the fact that he 'immediately instituted a senate with which to consult and according to the opinions of which he might form his resolutions', and because the only power he kept for himself 'was the command of the army in case of war, and the power of convok-

---

[7] *The Discourses*, Book I, Ch. I.

ing the Senate'.[8] Having discussed in the first part of this chapter
the behaviour of Romulus, the founder of a state, Machiavelli
turns in the latter half of the same chapter to the case of the
man who wishes to regenerate a corrupt state. It is clear from
Machiavelli's discussion that the same principles apply to the
regeneration of the corrupt state as to the founding of a new
one. It is best done by a single man, and evil means may be
justified by good results. Agis, King of Sparta, and Cleomenes
serve as the examples of men who attempt to regenerate a
state. Agis, perceiving that Sparta had fallen into corruption
by deviating from the laws of Lycurgus, attempted to bring the
Spartans back to a strict observance of them. He was promptly
killed for his trouble by the Ephores, who considered that he
was attempting to make himself a tyrant. His successor Cleomenes confronted the same problem, but saw that he must
possess sole authority in the state in order to reform it: 'he
judged that 'owing to the ambitious nature of men, he could not
promote the interests of the many against the will of the few;
and therefore availed himself of a convenient opportunity to
have all the Ephores slain, as well as all such others as might
oppose his project, after which he restored the laws of Lycurgus
entirely'.[9] Thus, just as the murder of Remus was justified by the
founding of Rome, so the murder of the Ephores is justified by the
regeneration of Sparta and Cleomenes deserved 'a reputation
equal to that of Lycurgus'. Toward the end of the following
chapter, Book I, Chapter X, occurs a sentence which again
implies that the task of one who would reform a state is the same
as the task of a founder. He has praised the good emperors of
history, those who were protected by 'the good will of the
people, and by the love of the senate' and has contrasted them
with those who like Caesar, ruined Rome. 'And truly,' he concludes, 'if a prince be anxious for glory and the good opinion
of the world, he should rather wish to possess a corrupt city, not
to ruin it wholly like Caesar, but to reorganise it like Romulus.
For certainly the heavens cannot afford a man a greater
opportunity of glory, nor men desire a better one.'[10] The first
thing to be observed about this passage is that, according to

[8] Ibid., Ch. ix.
[9] Ibid.
[10] Ibid., Ch. X.

Machiavelli's earlier discussion, Romulus did not *reorganise* a city, but rather founded one. Machiavelli thus argues that the two tasks are the same, that the man who founds a state and the man who reforms one should be governed by the same principles. Moreover, Machiavelli views the extraordinary means required for this task, such as the murder of Remus or of the Ephores, not with feelings of reluctance tempered by awareness of possible necessity, but as something to be *desired*. The 'heavens cannot afford a man a greater opportunity of glory, nor could men desire a better one'.

In these two chapters, then, Machiavelli begins the discussion which Bolingbroke was to resume in *The Idea of a Patriot King*, the discussion of the means required to found, or more pertinently, to refound, a state. The next five chapters of Book I, XI through XV, take up the question of religion, considered solely as a means of strengthening the state. Chapter XVI addresses itself to the difficulties involved in preserving newly acquired freedom in a state accustomed to living without it; but at the end of this chapter Machiavelli returns to the problem of the corrupt state, now introducing the question of the relationship between liberty, by which he means a government under law, and corruption. He points out that because the Romans were not corrupt they were able to recover their liberty and maintain it after the expulsion of the Tarquins, but that if they had been corrupt 'then there would have been no sufficient remedies found in Rome or elsewhere to maintain their liberty, as we shall show in the next chapter'.[11]

In the next chapter, XVII, Machiavelli at first appears to say that a people corrupted by bad rule can live in liberty if a good prince comes to power, but that when he dies they will revert to their former corrupt ways. The chapter heading reads: 'A Corrupt People That Becomes Free Can With Greatest Difficulty Maintain Its Liberty'. The opening sentences of the chapter assert the *impossibility* of regenerating a corrupt people in any lasting fashion:

> I think that it was necessary for royalty to be extinguished in Rome, else she would in a very short time have be come feeble and devoid of energy. For the degree of corruption to which the

[11] Ibid., Ch. XVI.

kings had sunk was such that, if it had continued for two or three successive reigns, and had extended from the head to the members of the body so that these had become also corrupt, it would have been impossible ever to have reformed the state. But losing the head while the trunk was still sound it was easy to restore Rome to liberty and proper institutions. And it must be assumed as a well demonstrated truth, that a corrupt people that lives under the government of a prince can never become free, even though the prince and his whole line should be extinguished; and that it would be better that the one prince should be destroyed by another. For a people in such condition can never become settled unless a new prince be created, who by his good qualities and valour can maintain their liberty; but even then it will last only during the lifetime of the new prince.[12]

Machiavelli supports this pessimistic view with the examples of Syracuse, which was restored during the lifetimes of Dion and Timoleon, but which after their deaths relapsed to the former tyranny, and of Rome, which 'after the expulsion of the Tarquins was enabled quickly to resume and maintain her liberty; but after the death of Caesar, Caligula and Nero, and after the extinction of the entire Caeserain line, could not even begin to re-establish her liberty, and much less preserve it'.[13] Machiavelli's analysis, so far, has this conclusion, which, however, he is to modify in the next paragraph: if a good ruler appears among a corrupt people he can restore liberty during his lifetime, but not regenerate the state; and, as soon as he dies, corruption will return. In a passage which finds many echoes in Bolingbroke, Machiavelli goes on to argue that 'faction', under the leadership of Caesar, was responsible for spreading corruption among the Roman people: 'This was the result of that corruption which has been spread among the people by the faction of Marius, at the head of which was Caesar, who had so blinded the people that they did not perceive the yoke they were imposing on themselves.'[14]

At this point in the chapter the issue seems closed, and Machiavelli repeats the conclusion he so far seems to have argued for: 'And although the example of Rome is preferable

[12] Ibid., Ch. XVII.
[13] Ibid.
[14] Ibid.

to all others, yet I will cite on this subject some instances amongst people in our own times. And therefore I say that *no change, however great or violent, could ever restore Milan and Naples to liberty, because the whole people of those states were thoroughly corrupt'* (italics mine).[15]

The finality with which Machiavelli states this conclusion, however, seems as we read further in the chapter to serve a primarily dramatic purpose. There is a way, he says, to regenerate even a state that has become corrupt. To do so requires a man of supreme power, a man greater, it may be, than any who have previously existed. This passage, which forms the conclusion of Chapter XVII, is of primary importance:

> . . . where corruption has penetrated the people, the best laws are of no avail, unless they are administered by a man of such supreme power that he may cause the laws to be observed until the mass has been restored to a healthy condition. And I know not whether such a case has ever occurred, or whether it possibly ever could occur (as I have said above). For if a state or city in decadence, in consequence of the corruption of the mass of its people, is ever raised up again, it must be through the virtue of some one man then living, and not by the people; and so soon as such a man dies, the people will relapse into their corrupt habits; as was the case in Thebes, which by the virtue of Epaminodes could, during his lifetime, maintain the form of a republic and its dominion, but immediately upon his death relapsed into anarchy. And the reason of this is that one man cannot live long enough to have time to bring a people back to good habits which for any length of time has indulged in evil ones. Or if one of extreme long life, or two continuous virtuous successors, do not restore the state, it will quickly lapse into ruin, no matter how many dangers and how much bloodshed have been incurred in the effort to restore it. For such corruption and incapacity to maintain free institutions result from a great inequality that exists in such a state; and to reduce the inhabitants to equality requires the application of extraordinary measures, which few know how, or are willing, to employ; as will be shown more fully elsewhere.

Now it is clear that this modifies to a considerable extent what has gone before in the chapter. It is not quite *impossible* to

[15] Ibid.

reform a corrupt state, though Machiavelli 'knows not' whether it has ever been done. The reason it may never have been done is that it requires 'extraordinary measures', and therefore a really extraordinary leader.

In the next chapter, XVIII, using the example of Rome, Machiavelli traces the progress of corruption, and argues that one method of preserving liberty there would have been to alter the constitution, which had been designed for an uncorrupted people. 'The constitution of the state reposed upon the authority of the people, the Senate, the Tribunes, and the Consuls, and upon the manner of choosing and creating the magistrates, and of making the laws.'[16] The former custom, therefore, of bestowing the consulate and other principal offices only upon those who asked for them would obviously be inappropriate to a corrupt people who were motivated no longer by public spirit. It follows that the way to preserve freedom would have been to change established customs in order to accomodate the changed spirit of the people. Such fundamental changes, Machiavelli says, can be accomplished either gradually or suddenly and through violence. In either case, he is pessimistic. 'For a gradual modification requires to be the work of some wise man, who has seen the evil from afar in its very beginning; but it is very likely that such a man may never rise up in the state, and even if he did he will hardly be able to persuade the others to do what he proposes; for men accustomed to live after one fashion do not like to change, and the less so as they do not see the evil staring them in the face, but presented to them as a mere conjecture.'[17] And, as for a sudden reformation, when the defect of institutions

have become manifest to everybody, that also is more difficult; for to do this ordinary means will not suffice; they may even be injurious under such circumstances, and *therefore it becomes necessary to resort to extraordinary measures, such as violence and arms,* and above all things to make oneself absolute master of the state, so as to be able to dispose of it at will. And as the reformation of the political condition of the state presupposes a good man, whilst the making of himself prince of a republic by violence naturally presupposes a bad one, it will consequently be exceedingly rare that a good man should be found willing to

16 Ibid., Ch. XVIII.
17 Ibid.

employ wicked means to become prince, even though his final object be good; or that a bad man, after having become prince, should be willing to labour for good ends, and that it should enter his mind to use for good purposes that authority which he has acquired by evil means. From these combined causes arises the difficulty or impossibility of maintaining liberty in a republic that has become corrupt, or to establish there anew. (Italics mine.)[18]

A careful reading of the relevant chapters from *The Discourses*, the principal passages from which we have been examining, yields the following conclusion, with which, in considerable part, Bolingbroke agrees. These chapters provide, indeed, the basis for Bolingbroke's formulation of the problem in *The Idea of a Patriot King*. According to Machiavelli, the re-establishment of liberty in a corrupt state, and the restoration of virtue among the people of such a state, is an extraordinarily difficult undertaking. It may be accomplished only by the rare individual who combines a willingness to use violence on a large scale with fidelity to moral virtue. He must, if necessary, be willing to reduce all to equality. He must be willing to imitate Romulus's murder of Remus, and Cleomenes's massacre of the Ephores, and indeed, Machiavelli intimates, go beyond them. At the same time, he must be willing to work for the public good, even when he has absolute power and all lies within his control. Still, according to Machiavelli, even when all this has been said, there may be a 'few' who meet these requirements.

Bolingbroke agrees, in *The Idea of the Patriot King*, that the saviour of a corrupt state must be an extraordinary man—a 'standing miracle' he calls him. And he admits that he must, under certain circumstances, resort to violence. But in Bolingbroke's treatment the role violence receives nowhere near the emphasis it does in *The Discourses*. In part this is due to the fact that Bolingbroke is writing for a legitimate king, one who comes to the throne by the normal process of inheritance, and who, furthermore, can depend on the existence of an aristocracy, however corrupt, whereas Machiavelli is considering one who must use evil means to 'make himself prince'. But, more than this, it is due to Bolingbroke's more optimistic estimate of human nature: his Patriot King employs the example of his own be-

[18] Ibid.

haviour to a far greater extent than coercion to rescue the state from corruption.

Apart from this difference in emphasis, however, Bolingbroke has a more fundamental criticism of Machiavelli which arises out of his interpretation of *The Prince*. In this contribution to the *de regimine* tradition, Machiavelli had attempted to define in an exemplary fashion the kind of extraordinary individual who would be capable of overcoming corruption and restoring the state to liberty and order. The Prince of Machiavelli would be a man of *virtu*, willing to use any means necessary to the accomplishment of his worthy goal, the reformation of the state. Like Henry Nevile and George Lyttelton, however, and like many others, Bolingbroke thought that he detected a contradiction between the problem as stated in *The Discourses* and the morality prescribed in *The Prince*. As Bolingbroke and others interpreted it, *The Prince* argues that the man of *virtu* need only *seem*, and not really *be*, virtuous. In concluding Chapter XVIII of *The Prince*, Machiavelli seemed to say just that:

> A prince must take great care that nothing goes out of his mouth which is not full of the above named five qualities, and, to see and hear him, he should seem to be all mercy, faith, integrity, humanity and religion. And nothing is more necessary than to seem to have this last quality, for men in general judge more by the eyes than by the hands, for every one can see, but very few have to feel. Everybody sees what you appear to be, few feel what you are, and those few will not dare to oppose themselves to the many, who have the majesty of the state to defend them; and in the actions of men, and especially of princes, from which there is no appeal, the end justifies the means. Let a prince therefore aim at conquering and maintaining the state, and the means will always be judged honourable and praised by everyone, for the vulgar is always taken by appearances and the issue of the event; and the few who are not vulgar are isolated when the many have a rallying point in the prince. A certain prince of the present time, whom it is well not to name, never does anything but preach peace and good faith, but he is really a great enemy to both, and either of them, had he observed them, would have lost him his state or reputation on many occasions.

In passages such as this, in which he suggests that it is the appearance of virtue that matters and not the reality, Machiavelli contradicted, Bolingbroke thinks, his own analysis in Chapter XVIII of Book I of *The Discourses*, in which he had asserted that his extraordinary man, to be successful in reforming the state, must possess genuine moral virtue, must be a *good* man willing to employ evil means. In the passage just quoted from *The Prince* Bolingbroke finds only the recommendation that the prince *seem* virtuous. It could be argued, however, that the virtuous qualities which Machiavelli wishes the prince to appear to have are the virtues of the private man, and that the principled political disinterestedness he found in Romulus is a virtue of another order altogether. On the other hand, it is clear that, for Bolingbroke, the difference between the private virtues and the public ones is not so clear as it is in Machiavelli, and in refusing to posit so sharp a distinction he was very much in harmony with traditional thought. This then is the first major point on which Bolingbroke bases his disagreement with Machiavelli, from whom he had learned much. *The Prince*, Bolingbroke thinks, fails at the precise point at which it breaks most dramatically with tradition, which had always held that a ruler should *exceed* his subjects in genuine moral virtue. *The Prince* fails, according to Bolingbroke, because it does not propose a genuine solution to the problem posed by Machiavelli in *The Discourses*.

The contingency which haunts Bolingbroke in his political speculations generally, and which becomes a central concern in his attack on Machiavelli, is defined by a passage in the Introduction to *The Idea of a Patriot King*. Bolingbroke recognises that the corruption of the state, if sufficiently advanced, may lead to 'universal confusion'. He fears that in such circumstances the man of *virtu*, owing allegiance to no principles which transcend circumstance, will not be very likely to forgo the opportunity of achieving absolute power. The problem set by Machiavelli, Bolingbroke thinks, is soluble only if, as traditional writers had maintained, and as Machiavelli himself had seemed to say in *The Discourses*, the prince *desired* to be subject to the law. For if he did not so desire, what would restrain him when the state was at his mercy? Castiglione had stated the traditional position when he said the ruler 'should form within himself and observe immutably in everything the law of reason, not written on paper or metal, but engraved in his very mind, that it may ever be to him not familiar but intrinsic, and that he may live with it as part of him'.[19] And Clichtoveus, to cite only one more example of a familiar injunction, had quoted approvingly from Claudian: 'Rightly you will have dominion over all things when you are able to be king of yourself.'[20] Following such writers as these in *The Idea of a Patriot King*, Bolingbroke opens his attack upon Machiavelli in this way:

> Machiavel is an author who should have great authority with the persons likely to oppose me. He proposes to princes the amplification of their power, the extent of their dominion, and the subjection of their people, as the sole objects of their policy. He devises and recommends all means that tend to these purposes, without the consideration of any duty owing to God or man, or any regard to the morality or immorality of actions. Yet even he declares the affectation of virtue to be useful to princes: he is so far on my side in the present situation. The only difference between us is, I would have the virtue real: he requires no more than the appearance of it.[21]

Here we have a clear statement of one of the major issues which, as Bolingbroke sees it, separates him from Machiavelli. Conceiving of virtue in traditional terms, Bolingbroke interprets Machiavelli's prince as basically amoral, and insists that morality is fundamental to the problem of the corrupt state as defined in *The Discourses*. He thinks that the man of *virtu*, as described in *The Prince*, possesses no inner check which would prevent him from seizing absolute power when the corruption of the state provides him with the opportunity.

Having pointed to what he considers a contradiction between *The Prince* and *The Discourses*, Bolingbroke goes on to define what, even in *The Discourses*, seems to have been omitted. He begins by paraphrasing the argument of Chapter X of the first book of *The Discourses*:

[19] '*Poi formi dentro a se stesso e osservi immutabilmente in ogni cosa la legge della ragione, non scritta in carte o in metallo, ma scolpita nell' animo suo proprio, accio che gli sia sempre non che familiare ma intrinseca, e con esso viva come parte di lui.*' (II cortegiano 4.23.)

[20]   '*Tunc omnia iure tenebis:*
                       Cum poteris rex esse tui.'
                              —Clichtoveus, *De regis officio*
                              4, folio 18 recto.

[21] *Bolingbroke*, II, 389.

In the tenth chapter of the first book of Discourses, he appears convinced, such is the force of truth, but now consistently with himself let others determine, that the supreme glory of a prince accrues to him who establishes good government and a free constitution, and that a prince, ambitious of fame, must wish to come into possession of a disordered and corrupted state, not to finish the wicked work that others have begun, and to complete the ruin, but to stop the progress of the first, and to prevent the last. He thinks this not only the true way to fame, but to security and quiet; as the contrary leads, for here is no third way, and a prince must make his option between these two, not only to infamy, but to danger and to perpetual disquietude. . . . He denies that such princes diminish their power by circumscribing it: and affirms, with truth on his side, that Timoleon, and others of the same character who he had cited possessed as great authority in their country, with every other advantage besides, as Dionysius or Phalaris had acquired, with the loss of all these advantages.[22]

With this argument from *The Discourses* Bolingbroke agrees, he says, completely, but he goes on to object that, valid as it is, it does not go far enough. 'Thus far Machiavel reasons justly; but he takes in only a part of his subject, and confines himself to those motives that should determine a wise prince to maintain liberty because it is his interest to do so. He rises no higher than the consideration of mere interest, of fame, of security, of quiet, and of power, all personal to the prince. . . . But he is far from going up to that motive which should above all determine a good prince to hold this conduct, because it is his duty to do so; a duty that he owes to God by one law, and to his people by another.'[23] What Bolingbroke is concerned to establish in this argument is that though moral laws may be observed to operate in the political process, these laws are rationally deducible, and that they are therefore confirmed by experience rather than merely arrived at inductively on the basis of inference. For all his scepticism, Bolingbroke remains the heir of the religious assumption that the universe is ruled by rational laws laid down by a benevolent Being, and that these laws are accessible, at least in part, to the human reason. Though he agrees, therefore, with what Machiavelli says about

[22] Ibid.
[23] Ibid.

the practicality of virtue in the passages he paraphrases from *The Discourses*, he would say, in contrast to Machiavelli, that such behaviour on the part of the ruler is not virtuous because it is practical, but practical because it is virtuous.

In the next section, before turning again explicitly to Machiavelli, Bolingbroke reflects briefly on the theory of the Social Contract as set forth by Locke, with which he agrees,[24] and goes on to draw a contrast between a good and a bad king. To set up a contrast was a familiar practice in the *de regimine principum* tradition, and like Bolingbroke most writers had followed, with various modifications, the contrast between the king and the tyrant as set forth in Aristotle's *Politics*. Boling-

---

[24] Ibid., pp. 390–1. Men were directed to form societies, Bolingbroke says, 'because they cannot by their nature subsist without them, nor in a state of individuality. . . .' It follows, according to Bolingbroke, that because society is necessary, government is too. Furthermore, he argues, good government requires liberty or else it will degenerate into tyranny, and therefore 'they are mutually necessary to each other, good government to support legal liberty, and legal liberty to preserve good government'. Both this passage and the rather peculiar one that follows it are perfunctory in their treatment of the issues they raise. One senses, in reading them, that Bolingbroke is anxious to proceed, as he soon does, with the further development of his main themes. For instance, Bolingbroke argues that men who, in forming society originally, submitted to tyranny have no rational recourse against it later. 'I speak not here of people, if any such there are, who have been savage or stupid enough to submit to tyranny by original contract; nor of those nations on whom tyranny has stolen as it were imperceptibly, or has been imposed by violence and settled by prescription. I shall exercise no political casuistry about the rights of such kings, and the obligations of such people. Men are to take their lots, perhaps, in governments as in climates, to fence against the inconveniencies of both, and to bear what they cannot alter.' Part of the difficulty here, evidently, is that Bolingbroke has conceived of the social contract as an historical phenomenon rather than as a metaphor contrived to rationalise the fact of obligation. In addition, his theory that societies are regenerated by returning to their original principles does not allow for the reform of societies whose first principles were bad, or which have been tyrannies so long that their first principles have been forgotten. On the other hand, these legalistic observations are not consistent with the opening paragraphs of *The Idea of a Patriot King*, in which, as we have seen, Bolingbroke argues that one can discover in one's own thoughts, 'according to the rule of reason', the principles of just institutions. It may be, however, that Bolingbroke has defined here, by virtue of the very inconsistency we have pointed out, a political problem which subsequent political philosophers have solved no better than he. In the societies he speaks of which have always been tyrannies we may see foreshadowed those countries which have no tradition of government by consent, and in which is has proved so difficult, if not impossible, to establish it. The rational institutions which, as Bolingbroke says, one may trace in one's own thoughts, require for successful installation some tradition of such institutions. They cannot be entirely alien. Here, then, may be part of the truth that is contained in Bolingbroke's conception of reform through returning to original principles.

broke's principal point in these paragraphs is the traditional one that according to the 'law of nature and reason, which has determined the end of government' the interest of the king and the interest of the people as a whole are the same. To this view, he says, another stands opposed, which holds that 'the king and the people in free governments are rival powers, who stand in competition with one another, who have different interests, and must of course have different views: that the rights and privileges of the people are so many spoils taken from the right and prerogative of the crown; and that the rules and laws, made for the exercise and security of the former, are so many diminutions of their dignity, and restraints on their power.'[25] This theory of the state, which Bolingbroke considered to be transcended by rational considerations common to *both* king and people, had been implicit in the works of Machiavelli. As did Madison in the tenth Federalist paper, Machiavelli viewed the state as in a condition of perpetual tension between the ruler and the ruled.

In his conclusion that the state is essentially a harmonious system, and that deviations from that harmony are the result of corruption, Bolingbroke was drawing the necessary conclusion from basically Aristotelian assumptions. Since the state is natural for man, that is, for the development of his specifically human capacities, and since all parts of the state function to promote the same end, the interest of the people and the interest of the ruler are ultimately the same. The state should be, Bolingbroke says, 'one system, composed of different parts and powers, but all duly proportioned to one another, and conspiring by their harmony to the perfection of the whole'.[26] These principles will be valid, Bolingbroke says, whether the king 'comes to the throne by immediate or remote election', that is, whether the monarchy is elective or hereditary.

In his conception of the harmonious state Bolingbroke considers that he does not so much contradict as go beyond Machiavelli. He is aware, of course, that as things go, in the market-place and in the forum, self-interest will play a large part in determining man's behaviour. On the other hand, just as when he previously argued that Machiavelli stopped short

[25] Ibid., p. 391.
[26] Ibid.

of the truth in urging self-interest and the desire for fame as the motives for goodness on the part of the king, Bolingbroke insists that a rational man—and he is not fully a man unless he is rational—will see that his most important interests are those which he has in common with his fellows. The common interest transcends the private one, since men cannot, as Bolingbroke says, subsist without society or in a state of anarchy.

At this point in his argument Bolingbroke evidently felt that he had pointed to the contradiction between *The Prince* and *The Discourses*, had demonstrated the insufficiency of the morality of appearances which, in his view, *The Prince* had set forth, and had shown that the ruler must be governed by principles which transcend self-interest. He next turns to a discussion of the need for the proper inculcation of these views in the prospective prince, and makes a number of interesting observations. But he has a further argument to raise in opposition to Machiavelli, which he takes up after the section on the education of the prospective prince. Referring to Machiavelli's analysis of the factors which make for 'the freedom of a constitution', which occurs in Chapter XVIII, Book I, of *The Discourses*, Bolingbroke says:

> The freedom of a constitution rests on two points. The orders of it are one: so Machiavel calls them, and I know not how to call them more significantly. He means not only the forms and customs, but the different classes and assemblies of men, with different powers and privileges attributed to them, which are established in the state. The spirit and character of the people are the other. On the mutual conformity and harmony of these the preservation of liberty depends.[27]

In the passage of *The Discourses* to which this makes reference, Machiavelli had argued that Roman liberty had decayed because, while the people were growing corrupt, the constitution had remained unchanged. He had argued that since the powerful were no longer restrained, as they once had been, by public spirit, and now used their power for selfish ends, reform would require that their power be taken from them, and all citizens 'reduced to equality'. Following Machiavelli, Bolingbroke observes that the 'orders' of a state may be 'essen-

[27] Ibid., pp. 393-4.

tially altered'—that is, change in their operation though not in their outward appearance—if the people becomes corrupt: 'these orders of the state may be essentially altered, and serve more effectually to the destruction of liberty, than the taking them away would serve, if the spirit and character of the people are lost'.[28]

Bolingbroke thus introduces his second major disagreement with Machiavelli, addressing himself to a particular circumstance set forth in *The Discourses*. Suppose, as Machiavelli had described this circumstances, the people have lost their former public spirit, and are now dominated by self-interest. Though the former structure of society and the older political forms remain intact, they no longer produce liberty as they once did. The nobles, it may be, are now the exploiters rather than the protectors of the poor. Under these conditions Machiavelli had recommended the revolutionary solution, though without holding out much hope of a successful outcome. The man of *virtu*, he had said, must reduce all the inhabitants to equality by employing extraordinary measures. Then, like a master sculptor with a mass of shapeless clay, he might re-create order, might refound the state. Machiavelli, as Felix Gilbert has said, conceives of his prince as an independent creative force rather than as the dependent member of a given moral order.[29] Bolingbroke, however, rejects this extreme solution, and points out that taking away the 'orders' of a state, that is, making a revolution, is very like to be destructive of liberty. The alternative that remains to Bolingbroke, who adheres to Machiavelli's analysis of the problem but rejects his solution, is for the prince to revive the spirit and character of the people so that the 'orders' of the state will once again function as they should. This is the solution that it is the principal task of *The Idea of a Patriot King* to advocate. Bolingbroke thinks that the condition of England under the Hanoverians corresponds to the description of a corrupt Rome given by Machiavelli in Chapter XVIII, Book I, of *The Discourses*. The constitution remains intact, but because the people have become corrupt, because an oligarchy has emerged which no longer fulfils the

[28] Ibid., p. 394.
[29] Felix Gilbert, 'The Humanist Concept of the Prince and *The Prince* of Machiavelli', *Journal of Modern History*, XI (1939), 487.

responsibilities of the aristocracy, liberty has decayed. But in contrast to Machiavelli, who advocates, in these circumstances, a revolution, Bolingbroke proposes to restore the national ethos without resorting to political reorganisation. It should be pointed out that in all of his arguments Bolingbroke assumes that the king will have come to the throne legitimately, and that the vestiges, at least, of an aristocratic structure of government remain. This assumption may account in part for his opinion that reform can be effected without dramatic *political* change.[30] Bolingbroke is thus a moral reformer and not a political revolutionist, though he recognises that if moral reform fails, and if, particularly, the ruling class cannot be made to fulfil its responsibilities, revolution will be the only remaining course.

In this critique there is a sense in which Bolingbroke functions as a critic of an academic tendency in Machiavelli's work. Elsewhere, in *On the Study and Use of History* he had charged him with generalising too widely from a limited number of examples. In the passage we have been considering here he criticises Machiavelli for leaping too soon to an *extreme* solution. Bolingbroke speaks here, one senses, out of his own experience of political power, and in a sense he is more sophisticated than Machiavelli. He knows, as did Burke, that extreme solutions generally sound better than they work, even though to certain temperaments—and no doubt Machiavelli's was one—the extreme solution has a certain aesthetic attractiveness, the ring of heroic realism and the suggestion that one has the ability to face the worst.

After a brief excursion into contemporary politics, in which he implies that Sir Robert Walpole has been responsible for corrupting public spirit in England, Bolingbroke returns to his own prescription for restoring it. He begins by paraphrasing and commenting upon the analysis from *The Discourses* which we have been discussing.

[30] See Hans Baron, *The Crisis of the Early Italian Renaissance* (Princeton, 1955). Baron shows the relationship between Machiavelli's thought and the tradition of republicanism which went back to the medieval communes: 'The belief in the democratic liberty of Florentine life, which had arisen in the wars for independence against Giangaleazzo and Filippo Maria, was darkened in the years of the Medicean principate. . . . In the late Quattrocento, when Medicean predominance over the Republic was swept away, the early Quattrocento conviction of the role civic freedom played in inter-state relations throughout history and in the internal life of Florence came again to the fore' (371).

Machiavel has treated, in the Discourses before cited, this question, 'whether, when the people are grown corrupt, a free government can be maintained, if they enjoy it; or established, if they enjoy it not?' And upon the whole matter he concludes for the difficulty, or rather the impossibility, of succeeding in either case. It will be worth while to observe his way of reasoning. He asserts very truly, and proves by the example of the Roman commonwealth, that those orders which are proper to maintain liberty, whilst a people remain uncorrupt, become improper and hurtful to liberty, when a people is grown corrupt. To remedy this abuse, new laws alone will not be sufficient. These orders, therefore, must be changed, according to him, and the constitution must be adapted to the depraved manners of the people. He shows that such a change in the orders, and constituent parts of the government, is impracticable, whether the attempt be made by gentle and slow, or by violent and precipitate measures: and from thence he concludes, that a free commonwealth can neither be maintained by a corrupt people, nor be established among them. But he adds, that 'if this can possibly be done, it must be done by drawing the constitution to the monarchical form of government'. 'accioche quelli huomini i quali, in qualche modo, frenati.' 'That a corrupt people, whom law cannot correct, may be restrained and corrected by a kingly power.' Here is the hinge on which the whole turns.[31]

As Bolingbroke correctly states his position, Machiavelli assumed that when a people had become corrupt the orders of the state ought to be changed, for without doing this it would be impossible to restore the national ethos. Bolingbroke replies that rather than changing the orders of the state, a ruler may revive the character and spirit of the people to the point where the traditional orders will be viable and the constitution can function properly. 'To preserve liberty by new laws and new schemes of government, whilst the corruption of a people continues and grows, is absolutely impossible: but to restore and preserve it under old laws, and an old constitution, by reinfusing into the minds of men the spirit of this constitution, is not only possible, but is, in a particular manner, easy to a king.'[32] Because he had such a pessimistic view of human nature, Machiavelli largely neglected this possible solution of the

[31] *Bolingbroke*, II, p. 395.
[32] Ibid., p. 396.

problem he had posed. Bolingbroke, on the other hand, seems insufficiently aware that under changing circumstances the institutions of a country may themselves have to be changed.[33] Nevertheless, in criticising Machiavelli, he was concerned to make the important point that the head of state can do much to improve the national ethos. One of the first, as we have seen, to systematically make use of literary men for the purposes of political propaganda, Bolingbroke had always been extremely sensitive to the possibilities of moulding public opinion, and he was fully aware of the importance of the 'image' projected by the head of the state.

In Bolingbroke's opinion, the means available to the Patriot King for rejuvenating the emotional ethos are several, but, like his humanist predecessors, he considered moral reform to be chief among them: 'Depravation of manners exposed the constitution to ruin: reformation will secure it.'[34] Like Swift, who made virtually the same proposal in 'A Project for the Advancement of Morality and Religion', Bolingbroke thinks the monarch can foster virtue by making it necessary to public advancement: 'by rendering public virtue and real capacity the sole means of acquiring any degree of power or profit in the state, he will set the passions of their hearts on the side of liberty and good government'.[35] In addition, the monarch himself is to set an inspiring example. For Bolingbroke, it is clear, the moral quality of national leadership took precedence over the specifically political measures which he does urge in later sections of the book. A monarch able to carry through such a reform is, Bolingbroke knows, a rare being; but he thinks that such a monarch provides the only solution, short of revolution, to the problem posed by Machiavelli and, by implication, by Walpole's England.[36]

[33] He is not, however, completely unaware of the possible necessity for change. He admits that the Constitution may require 'improvement', but insists that such important changes be gradual. The relevant passage on p. 402 of Vol. II is discussed in Ch. VII.

[34] *Bolingbroke*, II, p. 396.

[35] Ibid.

[36] Bolingbroke's recommendation that the monarch reform the manners of his people was familiar in the *de regimine principum* tradition. According to Aquinas, it 'is the king's responsibility . . . by his laws and instructions, by rewards and punishments, to keep from iniquity the men subject to him, and influence them toward virtuous deeds, taking his example from God, who gives law to men, and

Bolingbroke's prescription for the corrupt state as defined by Machiavelli in *The Discourses* followed the recommendation characteristic of the humanist tradition discussed in Chapter I. Bolingbroke differed from his predecessors only in applying their ideals to the particular problem set forth by Machiavelli. Whereas Machiavelli sees hope for curing the corruption of a state in the appearance of a prince who will by revolutionary methods reduce all to equality and refound the state, Bolingbroke returns to the traditional position in setting forth his conception of a disciplined and morally instructed Patriot King.[37] Yet even though he claims much for the concept of a Patriot King, Bolingbroke denies that even he can always ensure the survival of the state. Since states, like men, 'carry in them the seeds of their destruction', and since 'every hour that they live is an hour the less that they have to live', even a Patriot King can only delay what is inevitable.

We have been examining in some detail in this chapter Bolingbroke's analysis of an attack upon Machiavelli, which occupies the middle portion of *The Idea of a Patriot King*. In composing this manual, however, Bolingbroke employed the epistolary method which he customarily used in his treatises, and he therefore interrupts his remarks on Machiavelli from time to time to reflect upon other matters. Sometimes, for polemical purposes, he glances at contemporary English politics, viewing Walpole

---

[37] Machiavelli does not entirely ignore the possibility put forward by Bolingbroke in *The Idea of a Patriot King*. In the first chapter of Book III of *The Discourses* he says that a people may be 'brought back to themselves' either by changes in the laws or if 'some man of noble character arises amongst them, whose noble example and virtuous actions will produce the same effect as such a law'.

---

bestows a reward on those who observe them and penalties on those who transgress'. Other examples of this view are plentiful in classical writers on statecraft, and, as might be expected, humanist theoreticians repeated them. Clichtoveus pointed out that 'to whatever extent the life of a good prince furthers the pursuit of virtue among the people, to a like extent the wickedness of an evil king obstructs and hinders it' (*De regis officio*, 5, folio 21); and Erasmus likewise stressed the importance of the monarch's influence upon the moral temper of the people: 'There is no pestilence of which the contagion takes hold more quickly or spreads more widely than that of an evil prince. . . . Under a dicer there is a continual throwing of dice, under a warlike prince all are ready for war, under a spendthrift they give themselves over to luxury, under a licentious rule they become panders. . . . Turn over the histories of the ancients and you will find that the manners of any age were of the same sort as the life of the prince.' (*Institutio principis* I, 568F569B.)

as an agent of corruption, and linking him, by implication, with Machiavelli in common opposition to humanist principles. Bolingbroke also includes, in the vein of previous manuals *de regimine principum*, remarks on the proper education of the prospective monarch. He is concerned, as was Erasmus, that proper principles 'be sown as soon as possible in the mind of a prince, lest their growth should be checked by luxuriant weeds, which are apt to abound in such soils . . .'[38] He fears that unless proper principles are cultivated good government cannot be maintained or corrupt government reformed. In an interesting passage he compares the processes of education to those of nature. Our goals in education, he says, must be appropriate to our station in life, and all our efforts must tend toward the achievement of these goals:

> Thus we shall imitate the great operations of nature, and not the feeble, slow, and imperfect operations of art. We must not proceed, in forming the moral character, as a statuary proceeds in forming a statue, who works sometimes on the face, sometimes on one part, and sometimes on another; but we must proceed, and it is in our power to proceed, as nature does in forming a flower, and animal or any other of her productions; 'rudimenta partium omnium simul parit et producit'. 'She throws out altogether, and at once, the whole system of every being, and the rudiments of all the parts.' The vegetable or the animal grows in bulk and increases in strength; but is the same from the first. Just so our Patriot King must be a patriot from the first.[39]

What Bolingbroke evidently means here by 'natural' is *constant* or *habitual*. Like Burke, as has already been pointed out, he realised the centrality of habit to behaviour both political and personal, and his simile of the vegetable, growing in size but remaining the same, expresses very well his perception of the need for making principles *unconscious* as well as conscious. After one has fixed 'at once the general principles and ends of all his actions', and determined 'that his whole conduct shall be regulated by them, and directed by them', he will 'have turned, by one great effort, the bent of his mind so strongly towards the perfection of a kingly character, that he will exercise with ease,

[38] *Bolingbroke*, II, p. 392.
[39] Ibid.

and as it were by a natural determination, all the virtues of it'.[40] It is only when the principles discovered by reason have been made habitual, or unconscious, that they will be acted upon 'naturally', that is, with 'ease'.

In these remarks of Bolingbroke we may discriminate two different conceptions of the 'natural'. In the first place, there is the untrained or natural human mind. Bolingbroke speaks of its uncertain and irregular motions, and of its tendency some-times toward moral perfection and more often toward moral deprivation. But what Bolingbroke wishes to produce through education is what some writers have called man's 'second nature'. This is based on principles which may be arrived at rationally, and it orders and disciplines his untrained or first nature. Such a distinction was a traditional one and may be found most notably perhaps in Plato's portrait of Socrates. Arguing with his friends on the afternoon of his execution, Socrates explains his refusal to escape through the door his jailers have left open:

> . . . The Athenians have thought fit to condemn me, and accordingly I have thought it better and more right to remain here and undergo my sentence; for I am inclined to think that these muscles and bones of mine would have gone off long ago to Megara or Boeotia—by the dog of Egypt they would, if they had been moved only by their own idea of what was best, and if I had not chosen as the better and nobler part, instead of playing truant and running away, to undergo any punishment which the state inflicts. . . . It may be said, indeed, that without bones and muscles and other parts of the body, I cannot execute my purposes. But to say that I do as I do because of them, and that this is the way in which the mind acts, and not from the choice of the best, is a very careless and idle mode of speaking.[41]

Socrates distinguishes here between his physical organism, his first nature, to which he refers as 'they', meaning his muscles and bones, etc., and the 'I' which rules the entire organism. He, Socrates, is identified with the 'I' and he exercises what Aquinas was to call 'a royal and politic rule' over his 'irascible and concupiscible powers'. As against his friends, who would

[40] Ibid., p. 393.
[41] *The Dialogues of Plato*, trans. Jowett, II (New York, 1937), p. 483.

argue that it was only 'human' to run away, Socrates demonstrates what he considers the truly human by governing desire by principle. It is he, therefore, the man soon to be executed, who is truly fit to rule. Athens is not something external to him, and imposed upon him, but the end of his own truest character, that 'I' which is called Socrates. Unless all who have power partake of this process, Athens will degenerate into anarchy, each breaking the laws for the satisfaction of meaner motives.

The anti-Machiavellian arguments of *The Idea of a Patriot King* have two important functions. First and most evidently, they analyse and criticise some of Machiavelli's leading political ideas. Bolingbroke thinks, as we have seen, that Machiavelli is too pessimistic about the possibilities of moral reform, that he moves too quickly to the radical political solution. Bolingbroke takes this position because he is inclined to espouse a somewhat more benevolent view of human nature than can be extracted from the works of Machiavelli. He thinks, furthermore, that in cutting man off from traditional political norms Machiavelli casts him adrift in an amoral universe in which force and force only can prevail. In Bolingbroke's view, Machiavelli discards the norms of conduct which, rationally deducible and confirmed by experience, render man, though lower than the angels, yet higher than the beasts.

The whole problem of Machiavelli's intention in *The Prince* and *The Discourses* is an extremely difficult one, and experts differ widely in both interpretation of his work and evaluation of it. Those who have been involved with the problem, however, whether espousing sophisticated or relatively naïve positions, have divided, generally speaking, on the grounds defined by Bolingbroke. Writers who have praised Machiavelli—as patriot, as teacher of *realpolitik*, as social scientist, as psychologist—have almost invariably been hostile to or at least indifferent to the Classical-Christian moral tradition. On the other hand, those who have attacked Machiavelli from Elizabethan times through the present, down to Herbert Butterfield, C. S. Lewis, and Leo Strauss, have been part of, or sympathetic to, that tradition.[42]

[42] See Herbert Butterfield, *The Statecraft of Machiavelli* (London, 1955); Leo Strauss, *Thoughts on Machiavelli* (Glencoe, 1958); C. S. Lewis, *English Literature in the Sixteenth Century* (Oxford, 1954), p. 51.

But though Bolingbroke's anti-Machiavellian arguments can be extracted from their context in the manual and evaluated on their independent merits, they have, considered in context, an important ulterior function. Bolingbroke deliberately employed in *The Idea of a Patriot King* a form which, as we have seen, was characteristic of Renaissance humanism: the manual *de regimine principum.* As in the case of *Gulliver's Travels*, in its form and in many details affiliated with Rabelais and More, and of Gay's *Fables*, which recalls Aesop, and of *The Dunciad*, which echoes and alludes to the *Aeneid* and *Paradise Lost*, the *form* of Bolingbroke's manual calls to attention its connection with the cultural values of Renaissance humanism. By arguing that Machiavelli was hostile to these values, and then by connecting Walpole with Machiavelli, Bolingbroke was able to suggest that Walpole was not merely a clever, corrupt, and successful politician, but also the enemy of the central values of the humanist cultural tradition. Bolingbroke thus attempted a diagnosis of both the intellectual forces and the political-economic developments which were bringing to an end the humanist tradition. This diagnosis, expressed in Bolingbroke's manual as well as in *Gulliver's Travels* and *The Dunciad*, suggesting as it does that an entire cultural tradition is being menaced by Walpole, by the Whig oligarchy, and by the 'moneyed interests', endows these works of the Augustan humanists with their tragic power.

There is a further point to be made concerning this characteristic quality. We have seen that in his prescription for the regeneration of the state Bolingbroke follows the humanist tradition in counting on moral improvement, particularly in the case of the ruling class, and that he is inclined to take a more sanguine view than Machiavelli of man's capacity for moral reform. But he also has his doubts about this estimate. At times he seems to say that man is naturally inclined towards moral depravity. He thus entertains possibilities which are in a sense contradictory. Not nearly so optimistic as such predecessors of his as Erasmus, he puts forth the same political prescription. In *Gulliver's Travels*, likewise, Swift affirms humanist values, but at the same time adumbrates an Augustinian view of human depravity. Both writers—and it is a principal source of their irony—were employing humanist forms to express the awareness that humanist values were under attack, if not in the process of dissolution. Thus Swift both imitates and criticises Rabelais, and Bolingbroke, though he criticises Machiavelli, is fascinated by him and responds to his power. He is certainly not as certain as he sometimes seems that man's reason can exercise a royal and politic rule over his irascible and concupiscent powers.

VII

A MIRROR FOR THE
JUST PRINCE

I N the final section of his manual Bolingbroke attempts to apply his principles specifically to English problems. He shows how they worked in the past—Elizabeth, he thinks, was a Patriot Queen—and how the failure to apply them subsequently brought disaster; and he indicates how they may be brought to bear on current conditions. Thus he completes in this section the movement of his argument. He has argued, first, for the 'rationality' of his position, then refuted its most powerful theoretical antagonist, Machiavelli, and now he turns to the recommendation of particular measures.

In this concluding section of the book Bolingbroke attempts to adhere closely to the attitudes, and even to the specific advice, characteristic of his humanist predecessors. There are times, however, when he is forced to deal with matters in which they provide little guidance—with the rise of world trade, for example. It is clear, as we read these pages, that Bolingbroke is very much aware of the strains to which his humanist position is, ever increasingly, being subjected. Often the advice he offers is familiar enough: when the prince comes to power, he should purge his court of those who seem likely to be unco-operative; should pay attention to the pageantry appropriate to a court; from the very start should act decisively; should learn to distinguish wisdom in a minister from mere cunning.[1] Bolingbroke

---

[1] *The Works of Lord Bolingbroke*, II (Philadelphia, 1841), pp. 398–400. Bolingbroke's advice that the Patriot King should govern as soon as he begins to reign, agrees with the balance of typical opinion. Egidio had said, 'when opportunity for

has read Machiavelli carefully enough, however, and has had enough experience of politics himself, to know that even a virtuous ruler must sometimes employ disagreeable means: 'Wisdom and cunning may employ sometimes the same means too: but the wise man stoops to these means, and the other cannot rise above them.'[2] This resembles to some extent Machiavelli's advice that a prince must know, when occasion demands, how to act like a lion or a fox. But the emphasis Bolingbroke gives to his statement differs in an important way

[2] *Bolingbroke*, II, 399–400.

---

acting comes, if we properly desire to set and do not, it is because we are ignorant whether it is expedient that the deed in question should be done. . . . But after through daily consultation we rightly know what ought to be done; then if there is a chance to act we should act promptly.' Patricius quotes the proverb, 'slow in counsel, swift in execution'. Guicciardini agreed on the necessity for decisive action: 'tardiness in execution is much to be reprehended, when once a resolution has been made. . . .'

In noting the need for keeping up the pageantry of a Court, Bolingbroke touched upon a question which had been much discussed in manuals *de regimine principum*. The weight of opinion, at least since Aristotle, had been that rulers should be liberal. As Egidio puts it, following Aristotle, 'it is impossible for kings and princes to be prodigal, and . . . it is exceedingly appropriate for them to be liberal'. And others were even more emphatic, as were Patricius and Beroaldus. Machiavelli breaks with such advice, and subjects the question of liberality to a different kind of analysis. Parsimony, he says in Ch. 15 of *The Prince*, is less dangerous than poverty. Despite reservations and qualifications, Machiavelli's Prince is more cautious financially than the liberal ruler of the traditional manual. Bolingbroke's brief attention to the 'pageantry of a court' gives us no clue as to which side of this controversy he took, but does register his awareness of another of the subjects orthodox to such manuals as he was writing.

In his distinction between wisdom and cunning, as in his accompanying distinction between unlawful simulation and necessary but disagreeable dissimulation, Bolingbroke was in accord with most of the writers *de regimine principum*. As Patricius had said, 'The opinion of Agesilaus is well known, who says that not astuteness but excellence of goodness befits the kingly dignity.' Machiavelli's hero, in contrast, the Duke Valentino, the greatest of feigners—'grandissimo simulatore'—possessed just this astuteness, *astuzia*. In recommending it as, under certain circumstances, the highest of political virtues, Machiavelli was going counter to the moral disposition of tradition. Platina, for example, had written in more representative fashion: 'Astuteness is therefore to be put away. . . . For sagacity (as Aristotle holds) is the understanding of how to do things according to principles, for he thinks that men who possess that power are sagacious and good.' And Dante had made the same point in the *Convivio*: 'He is not to be called wise who proceeds by means of shady schemes and deceptions, but is to be called astute.' Bolingbroke's emphasis in this respect, as compared with that of Machiavelli, is in accord with the traditional attitude. Cunning must be used reluctantly, and while one retains a proper sense of its lower position in the moral hierarchy.

from that of Machiavelli: Bolingbroke admits the necessity reluctantly, always aware that the wise man 'stoops to these means'. Bolingbroke regards them as a deviation. He is anxious to maintain the traditional norms, which get perfunctory treatment in Machiavelli; he wishes to maintain the tension ethics introduces into politics.

Bolingbroke's description of the minister who is merely cunning seems to have been modelled on Robert Harley. 'The cunning minister . . . neither sees, nor is concerned to see, any further than his personal interests, and the support of his administration, require. If such a man overcomes any actual difficulty, avoids any immediate distress, or, without doing either of these effectually, gains a little time, by all the low artifices which cunning is ready to suggest and baseness of mind to employ, he triumphs . . .'[3] In Bolingbroke's view, Harley's lack of any larger political goals was the source of his failure: he seemed to be neither for the Tories nor for the Whigs, nor, in any clear fashion, for the Hanoverians or the Stuarts. In the *Letter to Sir William Wyndham*, for example, Bolingbroke had pointed out that Harley's indecisiveness concerning the larger issues cost him control of day-to-day events.[4]

The wise minister, in contrast, has more comprehensive views, 'sees, and is concerned to see, further, because government has a further concern; he sees the objects that are distant as well as those that are near, and all their remote relations, and even their indirect tendencies . . . He considers his administration as a single day in the great year of government; but as a day that is affected by those that went before, and that must affect those that follow.'[5] In reading passages like this it is difficult not to believe that Burke, though repelled by Bolingbroke's religious scepticism, was influenced by both the sub-

[3] Ibid., pp. 400–1.

[4] '[Harley] substitutes artifice in the place of ability, who instead of leading parties and governing accidents is eternally agitated backwards and forwards by both, who begins every day something new, and carries nothing on to perfection, [and] may impose a while on the world: but a little sooner or a little later the mystery will be revealed, and nothing will be found to be counched under it but a thread of pitiful expedients, the ultimate end of which never extended farther than living from day to day. . . . He hoped by cunning to varnish over his want of faith and ability.' (*Bolingbroke*, I, pp. 122–3.)

[5] Ibid., II, p. 401.

stance and the phraseology of Bolingbroke's writings on politics.[6]

Throughout the concluding part of his manual, Bolingbroke is concerned to stress the principle that the king must be above party. Assuming that various interests in the community will compete among themselves with varying degrees of attachment to the general interest, Bolingbroke sees that a crucial option is available to the ruler: will *he* use his position to aggrandise his own power and increase his privileges? Will he become identified, as Bolingbroke thought the first two Georges had become, with a single interest in the community? The problem to which Bolingbroke addressed himself remains, indeed, an important one. Today, as in Bolingbroke's time, it is essential that the executive preserve the disinterestedness of its relation to the community as a whole. 'There is a radical difference', as Walter Lippmann writes, 'between being a contender for power, a rival among rivals, and the guardian of the order which intends to regulate all the rivalries.'[7]

Care must be exercised, in interpreting Bolingbroke's references to party and faction, not to confuse his conception of party with the modern political organisations which are also called parties. Bolingbroke means by party a group held together only by its pursuit of a particular goal or its support of a particular interest:

> Parties, even before they degenerate into absolute factions, are still numbers of men associated together for certain purposes, and certain interests, which are not, or are not allowed to be, those of the community by others. A more private or personal interest comes but too soon, and too often, to be superadded, and to grow predominant in them . . . The interest of the state is supposed to be that of the party.[8]

The 'parties' Bolingbroke has in mind are not those which evolved during the nineteenth century, and which, though certainly representing particular interests in the community,

---

[6] Cf. 'Society . . . is a partnership in all science; a partnership in all art; a partnership in every virtue, and in all perfection. As the ends of such a partnership cannot be obtained in many generations, it becomes a partnership not only between those who are living, but between those who are living, those who are dead, and those who are to be born.' (Edmund Burke, *Reflections on the Revolution in France* (New York, 1951), p. 93.)

[7] Walter Lippmann, *The Public Philosophy* (Boston, 1955), p. 159.

[8] *Bolingbroke*, II, p. 402.

were more comprehensive in membership, and were informed, at least to some degree, by avowed principle. Parties in England during the first half of the eighteenth century were loosely associated collections of politicians held together by motives largely personal and local.[9] When Bolingbroke urged in the *Letter on the Spirit of Patriotism* that opposition to a bad administration had to be governed by principle, he was criticising in a similar vein the merely self-interested parties and factions familiar to him. Yet even though modern political parties are more comprehensive entities than those of Bolingbroke's time, they themselves may be criticised, in the manner of Bolingbroke, from the point of view of the national interest. 'We are party men,' said Winston Churchill to the Annual Conference of Conservatives in 1949, 'but we shall be all the stronger if in every action we show ourselves capable, even in this period of stress and provocation, of maintaining the division—where there is division—between national and party interests.'[10] And in the United States the fact that both major parties are actually coalitions, and do not represent a single class or section, tends to make them more responsive to the national interest than are the particularistic political organisations familiar in Europe, which are closer in essence to what Bolingbroke meant by 'faction'.

Swift agreed with Bolingbroke about the dangers of 'faction'. Lilliput decayed through the gradual increase of party and faction. Indeed, in a curious fashion, Karl Marx agreed, too. The Marxist revolution is to be brought about, and the state destroyed, by class warfare. The proletariat is, in Bolingbroke's sense, a faction, since it pursues power for the sake of but a single interest in the community.[11]

[9] Robert Walcott, *English Politics in the Early Eighteenth Century* (Oxford, 1956).

[10] Winston Churchill, *In the Balance* (Boston, 1952).

[11] Cf. *Bolingbroke*, II, 402. In his critique of party and faction, Bolingbroke followed the attitude of most Renaissance writers on the subject. Egidio, for example, had written: 'Tyrants wish to annoy friends with their friends, the people with men of rank, and those of rank with each other. For they see that when citizens are at variance with citizens and rich men with rich men, then correspondingly their power cannot be resisted, for since either party fears the other neither one rises against the tyrant. But on the contrary the true king does not procure disturbance among those living in his kingdom, but peace and concord. . . . The tenth device of the tyrant is that after he has brought about divisions and parties in the kingdom, he annoys one party with another that he may blunt

Bolingbroke recognises, however, that the Patriot King very likely will find that factions do exist in the state, and recommends various methods of dealing with them, the method to be applied depending upon the nature and causes of the division. Several of Bolingbroke's recommendations anticipate important principles of Burke. To reconcile opposed groups, for example, particular institutions may have to be modified, but such changes are best made slowly:

> As every new mortification in a scheme of government and of national policy is of great importance, and requires more and deeper consideration than the warmth and hurry, and rashness of party conduct admit, the duty of a prince seems to require that he should render by his influence the proceedings more

---

nail with nail. But the king on the contrary does not bring about divisions and parties in the kingdom, but if there are any he desires to get rid of them.' (*De regimine*, 3.2.10.) Aristotle, Patricius, and Erasmus adopted the same attitude: '*Hac animi perturbatione* [*discordia*] *quincunque civis laborat, inutilis est reipublicae, et in hominum coetu importunus habetur. Dissidet si quidem ab aliis, nemini cedit, omnemque humanam societatem dirimit, Principum sulas perturbat, Seditionibus, ac partibus omnia inficit; hinc conspirationes, coniurationesque oriuntur; hinc caedes, direptiones, veneficia, et postes illae teterrimae, quae status omnes publicos, privatosque labefactare solent. Crispi quidem Salustii sententia pro oraculo habenda est, quum ait: Concordia parvae res crescunt, discordia autem maximae dilabuntur. Per hanc interitum omnibus humanis societatibus parari scribit Xenophon.*' ('If a citizen has his mind perturbed by discord, he is useless to the state and is held dangerous in the society of men. If he disagrees with others he yields to no one, he breaks up all human society, causes disturbance in the courts of princes, infects everything with seditions and factions; thence arise conspiracies and plots, thence come murders, plunderings, poisonings, and those terrible plagues that overthrow all public and private establishments. Indeed, the saying of Crisphs Salustius should be considered as an oracle, for he said: "Little things through concord grow great, but great things dwindle away through discord." Xenophon says that through discord overthrow is prepared for all human organisations.') (*De regno* 4.10.) '*Tyrannus gaudet intercives factiones ac dissidia serere, et simultates forte fortuna obortas, diligenter alit ac provehit, atque his rebus* [*ad suae Tyrannidis communitionem abutitur. At hoc unicum Registudium est, civium rem inter eos componere, nimirum, qui intelligat hanc esse gravissimam rerum publicarum pestem.*' ('The tyrant delights in sowing factions and dissensions among his citizens, and rivalries that fortune happens to bring about he diligently nourishes and promotes, and these things he abuses for the strengthening of his tyranny. But it is the one effort of the king to nourish concord among the citizens and if any dissension should spring up, steadily to compose it among them, as one who knows that it is surely the worst disease of states.') (*Institution* I, 572 B-C.) Cf. Aristotle, *Politics*, III, xv, 9. Machiavelli, too, followed tradition in this respect. The ruler of *virtu* will, Machiavelli said, 'force the citizens to love one another, to live without factions, to estimate their private affairs as less important than those of the state'. The Duke Valentino, he says, like the virtuous Romans, took care that the State should be free from factions. (Cf. *The Art of War*, I; *The Prince*, Ch. 7.)

orderly and deliberate, even when he approves the end to which they are directed.[12]

In considering the merits of criticism, the Patriot King must also be able to distinguish 'the voice of his people from the clamour of a faction'.[13] What Bolingbroke means here by 'the voice of his people' is the genuine consensus of the community, interpreted in the light of its long-run interests. Burke agreed with Bolingbroke that the chief test of a genuine consensus was its steadiness as contrasted with transient fluctuations of feeling, and he agreed, too, that sudden changes were seldom in the general interest: 'Sure I am', said Burke, 'that no precipitate resolution on a great change in the fundamental constitution of any country can ever be called the real sense of the people.'[14]

When factions have become both powerful and violent, Bolingbroke admits, even a Patriot King may have to use force to re-establish public order.[15] Yet even when such violent factions have been put down, the king should not be vindictive toward those who composed them: 'if he is the conqueror, he will be the father, too, of his people', even though 'another prince' might choose a different course. The 'other prince' referred to here is undoubtedly the one projected by Machiavelli, who follows the advice that men 'will revenge themselves for small injuries, but cannot do so for great ones; the injury therefore that we do to a man must be such that we need not fear his vengeance'.[16] In his urging of clemency, Bolingbroke aligned himself with the advice traditional in the *de regimine* tradition, and thus again distinguished himself from Machiavelli.[17] Throughout his analysis of faction and its cure, moreover,

[12] *Bolingbroke*, II, p. 403.

[13] Ibid., p. 404.

[14] *Works*, Rivington edition, IX (1826–27), 321–2. Thomas Jefferson was of the same opinion and advised Lafayette against revolution; telling him to keep 'the good model of your neighbouring country before your eyes' and then to 'get on, step by step, towards a good constitution'. Quoted in Saul K. Padover, *Jefferson* (New York, 1955), p. 70.

[15] *Bolingbroke*, II, pp. 406–7.

[16] *The Prince*, Ch. 3.

[17] The subject of clemency occupied as important a place in previous works *de regimine principum* as it does in Bolingbroke's. The standard classical treatise on the subject, Seneca's *De clementis*, was often quoted in these works. Giraldus used Seneca's title as a chapter head, and argued at length that a prince should prefer mercy to cruelty: 'God himself in heaven detests cruelty and exhorts to clemency,

Bolingbroke alludes to the contemporary situation under George II: George and Walpole, he suggests, a weak King and an unscrupulous Minister, have exacerbated faction rather than dissolved it. Both the English Government, therefore, and Machiavelli are depicted as enemies of the traditional ethos embodied in Bolingbroke's manual.

Bolingbroke goes on to affirm, in an eloquent passage, the desirability of world government. 'Experience of the depravity of human nature made men desirous to unite in society and under government, that they might defend themselves better against injuries; but the same depravity soon inspired to some the design of employing societies to invade and spoil societies; and to disturb the peace of the great commonwealth of mankind, with more force and effect in collective bodies, than they could do individually.'[18] He compares factions in the state to nations in the world: both factions and nations 'invade and rob one another: and, while each pursues a separate interest, the common interest is sacrificed by them all'. Therefore, we infer, nations, like factions, should be as far as possible under a

---

[18] *Bolingbroke*, II, p. 412.

---

the first of which nature has assigned to beasts, the second to men.' Pontanus, Petrarch, Patricius, Rabelais, and Erasmus, to cite only a few, had urged clemency upon rulers. Nowhere, perhaps, did Machiavelli move more sharply from tradition than in arguing that a ruler's behaviour should be governed entirely by circumstances, and that sometimes, as in the case of Hannibal, 'inhuman cruelty' was justified. In his remarks on the subject of clemency, Bolingbroke takes the side of the traditional writers. Cf. '*Ipse autem ex alto crudelitatem detestatur, adhortatur clementiam, quorum alterum feris. alterum hominibus natura docuit assignandum.*' (Giraldus, *De principis instructione*, 1.7, pp. 25–27.) '*Sicut autem nulla re facilibus quam clementia, & liberalitate amor quaeritur plurimorum, sicecontra nil potentius ad odium concitandum, quam crudelitas atque cupiditas.*' ('As by nothing is the love of the many more easily obtained than by clemency and liberality, so on the contrary nothing is more powerful in exciting hate than cruelty and cupidity.') (Petrarch, *De rep. opt. adm.*, p. 428.) '*Clementiam in quo esse senserimus, illum omnes admiramur, pro deo habemus.*' ('When we have perceived that a man is clement, we all admire him, we look on him as a god.') (Pontanus, *De principe*, p. 257.) Patricius recommends in his chapter *De humanitate* '*benevolentia quaedam ac dexteritas erga omnes homines promiscam*' ('a certain benevolence and skill toward all men indiscriminately'). Erasmus observed, '*Tyrannus metui studet, Rex amari.*' ('The tyrant strives to be feared, the king to be loved.') (*Institutione principis*, cap. I, col. 572 B.) Gargantua's speech to the defeated followers of the defeated Picrochole in Ch. 50 of Book One, *Gargantua and Pantagruel*, is meant to be exemplary of a prince's clemency: 'Being unwilling therefore in any way to fall short of the hereditary graciousness of my parent, I now absolve and deliver you. . . .' (Cohen translation.)

Patriot King. Bolingbroke does not suppose that perfect harmony among nations can ever be achieved, any more than perfect harmony in the state; for 'private interest' must always in some measure affect 'the course of human affairs'. Nevertheless, a Patriot King can 'defeat the designs, and break the spirit of faction, instead of partaking in one, and assuming the other'. Thus if, as Bolingbroke has argued, the state was made necessary to end the Hobbesian war of all against all, a world society is necessary in order to end the war of all against all which prevails among nations. In part, no doubt, this passage in Bolingbroke reflects that Renaissance dream, reminiscent of Virgil and the *pax Romana*, but also reminiscent of the unified Christendom of the Middle Ages, which, during the Renaissance, was manifested as a series of visions of national empire. Just as Petrarch had projected a revival of the Roman hegemony, so Camoens saw Portugal as reconstructing European unity, and Ronsard and Spenser cast France and England in similar roles. The mantle of Rome passed from nation to nation.[19]

At this point Bolingbroke provides an historical example of a Patriot King, an example which had for over a hundred years been influential for the English political imagination. 'If these ends were ever answered, they were so, surely, in this country, in the days of our Elizabeth. She found her kingdoms full of factions, and factions of another consequence and danger than these of our days, whom she would have dispersed with a puff of her breath. She could not reunite them, it is true: the papist continued a papist, the puritan a puritan; one furious, the other sullen. But she united the great body of the people in her and their common interest, she inflamed them with one national spirit: and, thus armed, she maintained tranquillity at home, and carried succour to her friends and terror to her enemies abroad.'[20] The idealised memory of Queen Elizabeth's reign, it becomes clear, is one of the principal components of Bolingbroke's conception of the Patriot King. Indeed, it is not generally recognised how influential the memory of Elizabeth was

[19] See Etienne Gilson, *La Philosophie au Moyen Age* (Paris, 1947), pp. 193 ff.: '*La Transmission de la culture latine.*' The theme was a familiar one in England during the seventeenth and eighteenth centuries, as is shown by Aubrey Williams, *Pope's Dunciad*, Ch. II.

[20] *Bolingbroke*, II, pp. 412–13.

for the Augustan imagination. Bolingbroke, like Swift, traces 'the growth of faction' to the reigns of Elizabeth's successors. The passage on Elizabeth from *The Idea of a Patriot King* might, in fact, be taken as a synopsis of the political thesis of *Gulliver's Travels*. As Arthur Case has shown, both in Lilliput and Brobdingnag the 'grandfather' of the present ruler was meant to represent Elizabeth.[21] Lilliput, which indicates what England has become, degenerated from its 'original institutions' through 'corruptions' introduced by the grandfather of the Emperor now reigning, which 'grew to the present height by the gradual increase of party and faction'. Brobdingnag, which represents what England might have been had it retained its wise institutions, has been at peace since a general composition under 'this prince's grandfather' put an end to the struggles of faction. Thus Swift's account of English history is identical to Bolingbroke's.

Such use of Elizabeth as a polemical symbol against a present conceived of as disintegrating or corrupt was shared by the Augustan humanists, interestingly enough, with that least likely of groups, the Puritans. They, too, looked nostalgically back to Elizabeth's reign, and used it as a weapon in attacking contemporary conditions. Trevor-Roper, in an important essay, has argued that the Puritan rebellion was a rebellion of the landed gentry who were, throughout the early years of the seventeenth century, becoming increasingly impoverished. 'Puritan austerity was often the religion not of rich capitalists, saving to invest, but of poor gentry, saving to make ends meet. . . . It was appropriate that the leader of these gentry, when they became revolutionary, should have been Oliver Cromwell —the representative of a former court family, now reduced to their lands and obliged, in his youth, to sell their great house in Huntingdonshire to a new family. . . .' Such impoverished gentry, rebellious in temper, idealised the reign of Elizabeth, when, it was felt, they had been better off. 'Hence the cult, by the Puritans, not of new or mercantile or republican ideas, but of a vague, romanticised English monarchy such as they supposed had existed under the last sovereign of the old dynasty. "Queen Elizabeth of glorious memory." When the Independent Army reasserted itself and effortlessly drove out of power

[21] Arthur G. Case, *Four Essays on Gulliver's Travels* (Princeton, 1945), p. 111.

the little coterie of "whig" republicans who had usurped authority in its absence, the essential justification for that act was that the republican government thus overthrown was not, as it called itself, a "commonwealth", but "an oligarchy, detested by all men that love a commonwealth". And so Oliver Cromwell and his Independents replaced the policy of *laissez-faire* at home and mercantile aggression abroad against England's trade rivals, the Dutch, by an anachronistic revival of "Elizabethan" policy: paternal government, enforcement of poor and tillage laws, leadership of the "Protestant interest" in Europe, a protectorate over the Netherlands, a piratical war in the West Indies to tap the American treasure of Spain.'[22] The polemic carried on by Swift and Pope and Bolingbroke against some of the essentials of Puritanism, such as the 'inner light' and other anarchistic tendencies, may have distracted us from what they had in common with the Puritans. Both the 'Tory' humanists and the Puritans were protesting, in the name of a landed gentry which was being squeezed financially, against an increasingly powerful oligarchy. Both used the past as a weapon against this oligarchy, and both were revolutionary, either overtly, or implicitly, in some aspects of their programmes. Bolingbroke himself may have been aware of such resemblances between his own and the Puritan position, for he refers to Cromwell in *On the Study and Use of History* with more sympathy than one would expect. Cromwell's usurpation of power, he explains, was the consequence of a rebellion 'begun not without reason on account of liberty, but without any valid pretence on account of religion'.[23]

The power of Elizabeth as a symbol of unity is amply demonstrated by her use in this connection for such divergent positions as those represented by Donne, the Cromwellians, Swift, and Bolingbroke. Malcolm Ross has speculated that this power of Elizabeth was due to the fact that she represented, in retrospect,

---

[22] H. R. Trevor-Roper, 'The Social Causes of the Great Rebellion', *Men and Events* (New York, 1957), pp. 195–205. See also, however, Willson H. Coates, 'An Analysis of Major Conflicts in Seventeenth-Century England', *Conflict in Stuart England* (London, 1960). Mr. Coates, while admitting the usefulness of the economic analyses of both Trevor-Roper and Tawney, returns in modified fashion to the older 'Whig' view of the conflict: it really was, Coates thinks, primarily a struggle over religious and constitutional issues.

[23] *Bolingbroke*, II, p. 187.

that medieval synthesis of religion, ethics, and politics which had been shattered by the Reformation. A substitute for the Pope in an England which had separated itself from Catholic Christendom, she was both Head of State and Leader of the Church. Bolingbroke's conception of a united Europe under a Patriot King may be a faint echo, political and secular in its emphasis, of that older vision of unity. As Bolingbroke concludes his panegyric on Elizabeth:

> Let our great doctors in politics, who preach so learnedly on the trite text 'divide et impera', compare the conduct of Elizabeth in this respect with that of her successor, who endeavoured to govern his kingdom by the notions of a faction that he raised, and to manage his parliament by undertakers: and they must be very obstinate indeed if they refuse to acknowledge, that a wise and good prince can unite a divided people, though a weak and wicked prince cannot; and that the consequences of national union are glory and happiness to the prince and to the people; whilst those of disunion bring shame and misery on both, and entail them too on posterity.[24]

Bolingbroke agrees with Swift that after the death of Elizabeth England followed the course of Lilliput rather than that of Brobdingnag. 'The death of Queen Elizabeth,' he says in *On the Study and Use of History*, 'and the accession of king James the First, made a vast alteration in the government of our nation at home, and in her conduct abroad . . .'[25]

This section of Bolingbroke's work concludes with a paragraph which may be read simply as an attack upon Walpole and other of his political enemies. It is quite difficult, however, in view of the fact that *The Idea of a Patriot King* was conceived of as a theoretical work as well as an anti-Machiavel, not to consider this passage as applicable also to Machiavelli. By using such an innuendo, by bringing together the topical reference and the theoretical one, Bolingbroke could imply, as he had done throughout, that Walpole, like Machiavelli, was the enemy of traditional ethical values and not just a corrupt politician. John Gay and Swift had made the same charge in their printed works. According to Bolingbroke, there have always been crimi-

[24] Ibid., p. 413.
[25] Ibid., p. 250.

nals, but never, until now, men who argued that it was proper to be criminal upon principle:

> Hitherto it has been thought the highest pitch of profligacy to own, instead of concealing, crimes; and to take pride in them, instead of being ashamed of them. But in our age men have soared to a pitch still higher . . . the choice spirits of these days, the men of mode in politics, are far from stopping where criminals of all times have stopped, when they have gone even to this point; for generally the most hardened inhabitants of Newgate do not go so far. The men I speak of contend, that it is not enough to be vicious by practice and habit, but that it is necessary to be so by principle.[26]

In accordance with the established pattern for manuals of this sort, Bolingbroke next gives his monarch advice on foreign policy.[27] Though the ultimate interests of states are always the same, Bolingbroke argues, they differ in the manner of pursuing their interests because of variation in geography, climate, character of the people, and type of government. He urges that England, as an island, devote itself to a considerable degree to trade. Maritime power, he points out, is useful for trade, can be turned to military uses during wars, and makes it unnecessary for England to become involved in long and expensive wars on the Continent.[28] Thus, with considerable plausibility, he

---

[26] Ibid., p. 413.

[27] Machiavelli had taken this subject up in Ch. 21 of *The Prince*, and other writers *de regimine principum* also had included such advice in their manuals. For example, in his *Institutio*, Erasmus includes a chapter, '*De foederibus*', and another, '*De principum affinatibus*', and Diomede Carafa devotes considerable space to dealings with other sovereigns. The inclusion of advice on foreign policy is one of the things which, generally speaking, serves to distinguish Renaissance manuals for the prince, which had to take into account the problems of the nation-state, from earlier works of this sort.

[28] This section of *The Idea of a Patriot King* is analogous to Ch. 12 through 14 of *The Prince*, in which Machiavelli discusses such military matters as the value of mercenary soldiers as opposed to indigenous armies, the value of fortresses, and so forth. Other writers of manuals for princes had similarly taken up military policy. Egidio devotes to it one of the three parts of his third book. Frachetta divides his *Prencipe* (1599) into two sections, one on peacetime affairs, the other on warfare. Erasmus entitled one chapter of his *Institutio* '*De bello suscipiendo*,' but devoted it to discouraging the prince from undertaking conflict.

Bolingbroke, II, 419. Advice about the manner proper to a prince was familiar in works *de regimine principum*. Erasmus, for example, quotes in his *Lingua* Plato's advice that the speech of a ruler should be 'sparing in words, but impressive in the weight of opinion'. Giraldus Cambrensis urged: 'Therefore the prince, since he

urges a return to the principles of foreign policy that prevailed under the last Patriot monarch, Elizabeth, and which, indeed, he had tried to implement during his years of power under Anne.

In the final section of his book, now that he has discussed the possibilities of English domestic and foreign policy, Bolingbroke turns, as had Machiavelli and many other *de regimine* writers, to the prince's private life. He denies, contradicting Machiavelli—that a prince can succeed in seeming virtuous without really being virtuous:

> It is of his personal behaviour, of his manner of living with other men, and, in a word, of his private as well as public life that I mean to speak. It is of that decency and grace, that *bienseance* of the French, that decorum of the Latins, that πρεπον of the Greeks, which can never be reflected on any character that is not laid in virtue: but for want of which, a character that is so laid will lose, at all times, part of the lustre belonging to it, and may be sometimes not a little underestimated and undervalued. Beauty is not separable from health, nor this lustre, said the stoics, from virtue; but as a man may be healthful without being handsome, so he may be virtuous without being amiable.[29]

Just as true oratorical style is a reflection of the speaker's virtue, and just as the condition of the language is an index of the health of the culture, so a monarch's royal manner is related to the nobility of his soul. Ultimately, a monarch's style is as much a work of art as a poem or a painting. His manners must be given 'certain finishing strokes', a kind of polish, so that, like a perfect work of art, he will not appear 'defective because unfinished'. As Bolingbroke says, in 'moral characters, though every part be virtuous and great, or though the few and small defects in it be concealed under the blaze of those shining qualities that compensate for them; yet is this not enough even in private life: it is less so in public life, and still less so in that of a prince.

---

[29] *Bolingbroke*, II, pp. 419–20.

knows that he is as it were made into a conspicuous mirror on which the eyes of all are turned, is under obligation to restrain and control his mouth, his eyes, his individual limbs and all the movements of his body. . . .'

There is a certain "species liberalis", more easily understood than explained, that must be acquired and rendered habitual to him.' The prince's manners are not a mere façade. They are grounded in his moral character, but brought to perfection through art. Like a character in a neoclassical drama, the prince must 'neither say nor do any thing that is not exactly proper' to the character of a prince. Yet even a very good prince, one who tried to follow the advice of the traditional manual, Bolingbroke knew, might not be immune to minor vices. 'There goes a tradition that Henry the Fourth of France asked a Spanish ambassador, what mistresses the king of Spain had? The ambassador replied, like a formal pedant, that his master was a prince who feared God, and had no mistress but the queen. Henry the Fourth felt the reflection, and asked him in return, with some contempt, "Whether his master had not virtues enough to cover one vice?" '[30] But though Bolingbroke argues that minor vices may not be serious flaws in the character of a king, he makes an important distinction. The vices that may be covered or compensated for by more impressive virtues are 'those of the man, rather than those of the king; such as arise from constitution, and the natural rather than the moral character; such as may be deemed accidental starts of passion, or accidental remissness in some unguarded hours; surprises, if I may say so, of the man on the king'.[31]

The paragraphs which follow, and which conclude the main body of The Idea of a Patriot King, comprise a kind of 'mirror of princes'. Alexander, we are told, 'had violent passions, and those for wine and women were predominant, after his ambition . . . and, when he stood in all his easy hours surrounded by women and eunuchs, by the pandars, parasites, and buffoons of a voluptuous court, they, who could not approach the king, approached the man, and by seducing the man they betrayed the king. His faults became habits. The Macedonians, who did not or would not see the one, saw the other; and he fell a sacrifice to their resentments, to their fears, and to those factions that will arise under an odious government, as well as under one that grows into contempt.'[32] Scipio Africanus, on the other

30 Ibid., p. 420.
31 Ibid.
32 Ibid., p. 421.

hand, though lecherous, maintained as general, consul, and citizen the strictest ethical discipline, and as a result, 'with what panegyrics has not the whole torrent of writers rolled down his reputation even to these days?' Bolingbroke here dissents from the tradition of Scipio's chastity, embodied in the story of 'How hee sirnam'd of Africa dismiss'd / In his prime youth the fair Iberian maid'. Cato, Bolingbroke says, 'loved wine as well as Scipio loved women . . . but Cato's passion, as well as that of Scipio, was subdued and kept under by his public character'. It is difficult not to think that such passages as these, about the private vices of the great, contain a certain amount of autobiography. Both Julius Caesar and Caesar Augustus were lechers, Bolingbroke reports: 'Old Curio called Julius Caesar the husband of every wife, and the wife of every husband.' Augustus's panders ransacked Rome. That these men were tolerated, he argues, was evidence of Roman degeneracy. Yet Antony, who was no worse in deed, failed because he did not keep up appearances. 'I might produce many anecdotes to show how the two former saved appearances whilst their vices were the most flagrant, and made so much amends for the appearances they had not saved, by those of a contrary kind, that a great part at least of all which was said to defame them might pass, and did pass, for the calumny of party.' Not at all averse, we sense, to recounting some of his evidently inexhaustible store of anecdotes of royal vice, Bolingbroke concludes with the tale of 'a king of Achin, who is reported to have passed his whole time in a seraglio, eating, drinking, chewing betel, playing with women, and talking of cock fighting'.[33] Though perfection of the princely character, we gather, requires true inner virtue, the vices one may in some sense tolerate are those of the flesh, the private ones. Thus the king, as a public functionary, must be more moral than the man who fills the role.

The public styles of monarchs differ from one country to another, Bolingbroke says, according to the 'constitutions of governments, and the different tempers and characters of people'. Some of the profiles he gives here of various rulers are witty and amusing. Louis's successor, he says, was 'a mere rake, with some wit, and no morals'. Elizabeth governed, as was appropriate in a limited monarchy, 'by affection'.

[33] Ibid., p. 423.

Popularity was . . . the sole true foundation of that sufficient authority and influence. . . . The wise queen saw . . . how much popularity depends on those appearances, that depend on the decorum, the decency, the grace and the propriety of behaviour of which we have been speaking . . . she never suffered her friends to forget she was their queen; and when her favourites did, she made them feel that she was so.[34]

In contrast to Elizabeth, James I had no virtues but many weaknesses. Not 'having one quality to conciliate the esteem or affection of his people to him, [he] endeavoured to impose on their understandings', by spreading the doctrine of the divine rights of kings. He 'figured in church controversies, and put on all the appearances of a scholar, whilst he neglected all those of a great and good man, as well as king'. In his discussion of James, Bolingbroke echoes the treatment by many previous writers of the ways in which a monarch may bring himself into contempt.[35]

[34] Ibid., p. 425.

[35] Aristotle discussed the kind of behaviour which brings monarchs into contempt and helps to cause revolutions (*Politics*, V). The subject was a favourite one among writers *de regimine principum*. Platina: '*Facile enim contemnuntur, qui nihil habent, quique nec sibi nec alteri posunt, ut dicitur, contra vero in admiratione, omnium sunt, qui anteire caeteros virtute putantur, atque iis vitiis carere quibus alii non facile possunt obsistere. Hos admirantur populi, hos amant, hos colunt ut Deos, fieri enim non potest, ut eum contemnam, quem video enti, curare, ut omnes quam beatissime vivant.*' ('For they are easily contemned who have nothing of virtue, nothing of spirit, nothing of vigour, and they are of no avail either to themselves or others, as it is put; but on the contrary those who are thought to exceed others in virtue and to lack those vices which others cannot easily resist are admired by every one. The people admire them, love them, revere them as gods, for it cannot be that I should despise a man whom I see exerting himself and taking precautions that all may live as happily as possible.') (*Principis diatuposis*, 1.12.)

Bizzarus: '*Contemptus potissimum provenit, si voluptati, luxui, ac intemperantiae dedatur, ex quo etiam fit, ut nascatur odium si quid crudele interseratur, si frequentioribus conviviis et lusibus oblectetur, si stultis ac histrionibus raveat, si stupidi sint et amentes, si etiam sint molles ac effeminati, ut olim Sardanapalus, qui ob id Regnum amisit.*' ('Contempt most easily rises if he is given to pleasure, luxury, and intemperance; contempt may give birth to hatred if some cruelty is intermixed, if he is entertained by too frequent banquets and shows, if he favours base men and actors, if he is stupid and foolish, if he is soft and effeminate, as once Sardanapalus was, who because of it lost his kingdom.') (*De optimo principe*, p. 10 recto.)

Many other examples, of course, could be given of advice in this vein. Machiavelli entitles his Ch. 19 '*De contemptu et odio fugiendo*' ('Of escaping contempt and hatred.') He says that contempt is the result of a king's being considered variable, light, effeminate, poor spirited, irresolute, and that contempt can be avoided by greatness, courage, gravity and fortitude. In Shakespeare's *Henry IV*, Part I, Bolingbroke's description of the behaviour of Richard II is in this vein.

Bolingbroke concludes his advice to the prince with a section devoted to maxims, to such traditional advice as that a 'prince should choose his companions with as great care as his ministers'. Some of these maxims are very well phrased, as in the case of the one treating licentiousness of behaviour: 'Ceremony is the barrier against this abuse of liberty in public; politeness and decency are so in private.' He advises, in the customary vein, but with evident reference to the relations of George II and Walpole, that the king should not let his minister stand between him and the people, nor should his conduct be influenced by his favourites. For the most part, these highly polished maxims represent the conventional, but sound, attitudes of the typical manual for the prince.

In his conclusion Bolingbroke returns to the themes he began with. His analysis, he says, has been 'founded on true propositions, all of which are obvious . . . They are confirmed by universal experience.' And he identifies, by reference to Plato, the classical political tradition to which he belongs: 'let the imagination range through the whole glorious scene of a patriot reign; the beauty of the idea will inspire those transports, which Plato imagined the vision of virtue would inspire, if virtue could be seen.' And in his closing sentence he refers to Virgil, whom he views as the celebrant of universal order, an order such as a Patriot King might institute: of a Patriot King,

> and of such a prince alone, it may be said with strict propriety and truth, '*Volentes/ Per populos dat jura, viamque affectat Olympo.*' Civil fury will have no place in this draught: or, if the monster is seen, he must be seen as Virgil describes him, '*Centum vinctus ahensis/ Post tergum nodis, fremit horridus ore creento.*' He must be seen subdued, bound, chained, and deprived entirely of power to do hurt. In his place, concord will appear, brooding peace and prosperity on the happy land; joy sitting in every face, content in every heart; a people unoppressed, undisturbed, unalarmed; busy to improve their private property and the public stock; fleets covering the ocean, bringing home wealth by the returns of industry, carrying assistance or terror abroad by the direction of wisdom, and asserting triumphantly the right and the honour of Great Britain, as far as waters roll and as winds can waft them.[36]

[36] *Bolingbroke*, II, p. 429.

Bolingbroke's concluding exhortation contrasts in significant ways with that of *The Prince*. Chapter 26 of *The Prince* which corresponds to Bolingbroke's conclusion, asks for the liberation of Italy from foreign domination, and urges the Medici to take up this task. It is, accordingly, concerned in large part with military matters. The Prince it envisions will be a warrior: if 'it always seems as if military capacity were extinct, this is because the ancient methods were not good, and no one has arisen who knew how to discover new ones'. Machiavelli culminates his exhortation with an analysis of the military weaknesses of the Spaniards, French, and Swiss, and ends with a verse from Petrarch: let the 'combat be quickly sped'. This conclusion contrasts sharply with the Virgilian conclusion of Bolingbroke, with its evocation of universal peace. It might validly be said that the contrast is due to the problem to which Machiavelli addressed himself, that of freeing Italy from foreign domination, 'which stinks in the nostrils of everyone'—primarily a military problem. But even so, he might have concluded with a vision of the order which would prevail when the foreigners had been expelled. The difference between Bolingbroke's conclusion and the last chapter of *The Prince* is not, I think, entirely due to the topical problems which engrossed the two writers, but rather reflects a philosophical difference which has run through all their disagreements.

For Machiavelli, the world is not ruled by the decrees of a rational providence, but is rather in a state of flux. Envisioning only flux, he must in honesty advise his prince how to live in such a world. His controlling images are images of combat: Fortune must be conquered by force, he says, overcome by the bold, mastered by audacity. Caesare Borgia, at the summit of his career, erred—and 'was thrown aside by fortune'. For Machiavelli, therefore, war is not merely necessary in order to liberate Italy, it is in a sense the very condition of politics. The criterion of a prince of genuine *virtu* is his ability to wage war not only on the battlefield but, finally, with the condition of the universe itself. It is appropriate, therefore, that *The Prince* conclude with an exhortation to combat.

Implicit in the work of Bolingbroke is an entirely different view. No matter how much he learns from Machiavelli, no matter how frequently he imitates him, it is this difference which controls his allegiance to tradition at all decisive points. For Bolingbroke, the universe is not ultimately characterised by flux but by a rational and ultimately moral order. This order is not, in large part, entirely intelligible to man. But it *is* partially intelligible, intelligible enough for man to deduce that harmony is its essential characteristic. Complete harmony in political affairs may never be achieved, but man knows that he is moving toward an accord with the nature of things as he moves toward harmony. If for Machiavelli, *virtu* is the ability to wage successful combat, Bolingbroke's virtuous man is a man of peace. It is for this reason that the culmination of his political vision is expressed in images of harmony and world empire. Moreover, as we have seen, Bolingbroke's prince is one who responds, as far as possible, to a conception of what is appropriate to the *idea* of a ruler. Circumstance may impinge upon him, but principle, which never changes, impinges upon circumstance. The idea of a prince is a permanent thing, because principle is permanent. Machiavelli's prince is governed by circumstance: magnanimity may be called for, but then again it may not be; and the same for the other traditional virtues.

EPILOGUE

SOME of the most perceptive remarks yet made on Boling-broke appear in G. K. Chesterton's *A Short History of England*. Chesterton sees what other historians have missed: that Boling-broke's career, whether one considers his political or his intellectual activity, should be understood as an attempt to preserve a variety of traditional values during a period of drastic social and intellectual change. Bolingbroke disliked the idea that politics or economics could be separated from ethics; it was, however, Mandeville's doctrine of utility that adumbrated the controlling attitudes of the nineteenth century. Bolingbroke diagnosed correctly the causes of social disruption in his century, saw that the rising oligarchy would displace much that had been valuable in traditional English life. Signs were not lacking even during his lifetime that England was to become 'two nations'. Awareness of this central conservative purpose and of the difficulties attendant upon it should serve as the basis of any attempt to explain either his apparently erratic political behaviour or the ambivalent character of some of his principal intellectual endeavours.

He was, as we have seen, a humanist in the Renaissance sense, and he felt the force of the traditional conception of political ethics; but he was also Machiavelli's most important English disciple. He disliked the moneyed interest and the ethics of the trading classes, but he knew that trade must play an increasingly important part in the British economy, and he attempted to come to terms with that fact in his political theory. He possessed aristocratic tastes in literature, and his most famous book is in a traditional genre, the manual for the prince; but he sensed more profoundly than any individual of his time the immense advantages propaganda could give to the politician who made use of it. Then, too, he celebrated, at a time when important departments of culture were passing under the aegis of the specialist, the Renaissance ideal of the educated gentleman, the man whose judgment in matters of public moment might be trusted because in at least a general way he had intellectual command of an entire culture.

Bolingbroke's notorious religious views also exhibit the characteristic stresses of his position. Unlike Swift and Pope, with whom he agreed on political and cultural matters, Bolingbroke was not a Christian, though he certainly did believe in the existence of God and in his wisdom and justice. Yet if Bolingbroke could not, given his neoclassical commitment to general laws, believe in the validity of a particular revelation, his moral and political thought retains a Christian colouring, as in the language he uses to describe his projected political saviour, the Patriot King.

I think that today we are more likely than preceding generations to respond sympathetically to Bolingbroke, to understand the quality of the dilemmas he faced. Bolingbroke stressed the importance of a rational ethical basis for politics, and we are once again concerned to define such a basis, if the number of books which have appeared recently on the subject of Natural Law may be taken as indicative. Bolingbroke thought that he knew what was 'rational', and what was 'human', and considered that he could define the sort of society which was hospitable to those qualities. We are, to be sure, far less confident of such formulations than he was, but to a greater degree than in the recent past we feel the need for them. Bolingbroke also directed attention to the importance of leadership in the state, now once more the subject of serious discussion after a long period during which it was fashionable to attribute all historical efficacy to impersonal forces. The very pressure of specialisation, the increasing complexity of culture, has drawn attention once more to the importance of the generally educated man. But perhaps it is the central tendency of Bolingbroke's thought, rather than any particular aspect of it, that will prove most sympathetic to us. More aware than his victorious opponents of the pathos of history, he worked to preserve, in a period of change that was to a considerable degree destructive, what was most valuable in his cultural tradition.

INDEX